WILLIAMS-SONOMA

SEAFOOD

RECIPES AND TEXT
CAROLYN MILLER

GENERAL EDITOR
CHUCK WILLIAMS

PHOTOGRAPHS
MAREN CARUSO

SIMON & SCHUSTER • **SOURCE**

NEW YORK • LONDON • TORONTO • SYDNEY

CONTENTS

THE CLASSICS

QUICK DINNERS

SEAFOOD IN THE OVEN

SUMMER GRILLING

SOUPS AND STEWS

SPECIAL OCCASIONS

INTRODUCTION

Preparing seafood can entail nothing more than shucking a fresh oyster to enjoy with a tangy citrus mignonette sauce. Even the most traditional seafood dishes, such as boiled lobster with drawn butter or poached salmon with dill sauce, are remarkably easy to prepare, yet yield impressive and delicious results. Whether grilled, panfried, roasted, steamed, or simmered in a rich stew or chowder, simply prepared fish and shellfish is a boon for every cook.

We'd like to share some of these simple but versatile seafood dishes with you in these pages. An informative basics section at the back of the book provides indispensable tips, including how to choose the freshest seafood and prevent it from becoming overcooked. From the flavorful French dish of mussels marinière to fragrant Spanish seafood paella to a quick Asian stir-fry with shrimp and asparagus, every culture has its favorite seafood dishes. I urge you to try each of the recipes in this book to discover your own favorites, which I hope will appear time and again on your table.

Chuck Williams

THE CLASSICS

From simple yet luxurious oysters on the half shell to rich lobster Thermidor, the recipes that follow are favorites that have stood the test of time. The appetizers and main courses in this chapter include a flavorful French dish of mussels cooked in white wine, as well as that American seaboard favorite, crab cakes.

OYSTERS ON THE HALF SHELL WITH CITRUS MIGNONETTE SAUCE

To make the sauce, in a small bowl, combine the vinegar, tangerine zest and juice, shallot, and watercress. Season with salt and pepper to taste. Stir to blend.

Fill a large shallow bowl or 4 shallow soup bowls with crushed ice. Pour the sauce into 4 separate small bowls.

Place a shucked oyster in each of the reserved bottom shells. Nestle the oysters on the half shell in the crushed ice. Garnish the ice with the watercress sprigs. Serve immediately with a bowl of the sauce alongside, so that diners can spoon a teaspoonful of the sauce onto each oyster before eating it.

Note: The classic French mignonette sauce served with oysters on the half shell is a mixture of vinegar, shallots, salt, pepper, and another acidic liquid such as wine or lemon juice. The sauce takes its name from the French term for coarsely ground pepper.

MAKES 4 FIRST-COURSE SERVINGS

SHUCKING OYSTERS

Shucking oysters requires the right tools and some patience. You will need an oyster knife and a heavy glove or oven mitt. Hold the oyster in your gloved hand, rounded side down and pointed end toward you. Insert the knife tip under the hinge, in the small indention between the upper and lower shells. Move the knife away from the hinge and twist until the shell cracks open. Move the knife toward the rounded end to cut the top connector muscle, and twist off the top shell. Run the knife under the oyster to sever the bottom connector muscle.

FOR THE CITRUS MIGNONETTE SAUCE:

½ cup (4 fl oz/125 ml) Champagne vinegar

Grated zest and juice of 1 large tangerine, blood orange, or Valencia orange

1 shallot, minced

2 tablespoons minced watercress or fresh flat-leaf (Italian) parsley

Sea salt and freshly ground pepper

Crushed ice for serving

16 large or 24 small oysters, scrubbed and shucked *(far left),* deeper bottom shells reserved

Watercress or fresh flat-leaf (Italian) parsley sprigs for garnish

MUSSELS MARINIÈRE

4 tablespoons (2 oz/60 g) unsalted butter

3 cloves garlic, minced

2 large shallots, minced

1 small leek, white part only, finely chopped

1 tablespoon minced fresh thyme, or 1 teaspoon dried thyme, crumbled

Grated zest of 1 lemon

1 bay leaf

2 lb (1 kg) large black mussels, rinsed and debearded (far right)

1 cup (8 fl oz/250 ml) dry white vermouth or wine

Juice of 1 lemon

Freshly ground pepper

½ cup (¾ oz/20 g) minced fresh flat-leaf (Italian) parsley

Thick slices coarse country bread, lightly toasted, for serving

In a large, heavy nonreactive saucepan over medium heat, melt 2 tablespoons of the butter. Add the garlic, shallots, leek, thyme, lemon zest, and bay leaf. Sauté until the shallots and leek are translucent, about 3 minutes. Add the mussels to the pan, discarding any that do not close to the touch, and pour the vermouth over them. Cover and raise the heat to high. Cook, shaking the pan with one hand and holding the lid on with the other, until the mussels have opened, 4–5 minutes. Discard any mussels that do not open. Discard the bay leaf.

Turn off the heat and add the remaining 2 tablespoons butter to the liquid in the pan. Shake the pan gently until the butter melts. Stir in the lemon juice and sprinkle generously with pepper. Sprinkle the parsley over the mussels and shake the pan again.

Using a slotted spoon, divide the mussels among 4 warmed deep soup bowls. Pour the pan liquid over the mussels, dividing it equally among the bowls, and serve immediately with the toasted bread for dipping into the liquid.

MAKES 4 MAIN-COURSE SERVINGS

PREPARING MUSSELS

Mussels are usually sold soaked and scrubbed to remove any sand, and many of them come without the stringy "beards" that hold the mussels onto rocks. Simply rinse the mussels under cold running water and, if necessary, pull off the beards just before cooking. Mussels should be alive when cooked. Some fish stores will let you pick out your own mussels; if this is not the case, ask your fishmonger to check through the mussels individually and discard any that do not close to the touch, an indication that they are already dead. Discard any mussels that do not open after cooking.

CRAB CAKES WITH LEMON AIOLI

To make the aioli, using a mortar and pestle, grind the garlic and a pinch of salt together. Add the egg yolk and whisk until thick and sticky, about 15 seconds. Gradually whisk in the canola oil, a drop at a time until the sauce thickens, and then in a thin stream. Whisk in the olive oil and then the lemon zest and lemon juice. Season with salt and pepper. Add more lemon juice, if desired.

Pick over the crabmeat for shell fragments and drain in a sieve for up to 15 minutes, if needed. In a bowl, combine the crabmeat, chives, shallot, celery, crème fraîche, lemon zest, and Tabasco sauce, salt, and pepper to taste. Gently stir to combine. In a deep bowl, whisk the egg white until stiff peaks form, then fold the egg white into the crab mixture. Place the cornmeal in a shallow bowl.

Form ⅓ cup (1½ oz/45 g) of the crab mixture into a flat patty. Repeat with the remaining mixture to make 6 crab cakes, placing each on a small baking sheet. Using a metal spatula, transfer each crab cake to the bowl of cornmeal and carefully turn to coat evenly on all sides. Return the cakes to the baking sheet and refrigerate for 1 hour; this will help them hold together when fried.

In a large frying pan over medium heat, heat about ¼ inch (6 mm) canola oil until the oil shimmers. Add the cakes in batches and fry until golden, 1–2 minutes on each side. Keep the crab cakes warm in a 200°F (95°C) oven while frying the remaining cakes.

In a medium bowl, whisk together the olive oil and lemon juice until blended. Add the watercress and toss to coat. Add salt and pepper to taste and toss again. Divide the dressed greens among 3 salad plates or 2 dinner plates. Divide the crab cakes over the greens and top each with a dollop of lemon aioli. Serve at once.

Note: Aioli contains uncooked egg; see page 113.

MAKES 3 FIRST-COURSE SERVINGS OR 2 MAIN-COURSE SERVINGS

MAKING AIOLI

Aioli, the garlic mayonnaise of Provence, accompanies everything from crudités to fish soup. Like mayonnaise, aioli may be made in a blender (using a whole egg instead of a yolk). It is easy, though, to make aioli by hand. Just remember to beat the egg yolk before adding the oil, and to add the oil to the yolk *very* slowly at first—a few drops at a time—so that the yolk can absorb the oil and form a smooth blend. If your aioli separates, beat a tablespoon of it with a teaspoon prepared mustard in a warmed bowl, and beat in the broken aioli a tablespoon at a time until it thickens.

FOR THE LEMON AIOLI:

1 clove garlic

Sea salt and white pepper

1 egg yolk (see Note)

⅓ cup (3 fl oz/80 ml) canola or grapeseed oil

2 tablespoons extra-virgin olive oil

Grated zest of 1 lemon

1 tablespoon fresh lemon juice, or to taste

½ lb (250 g) fresh lump crabmeat

1 tablespoon minced chives

1 shallot, minced

¼ cup (1½ oz/45 g) finely diced celery

2 tablespoons crème fraîche or sour cream

Grated zest of 1 lemon

Tabasco sauce

1 egg white

Cornmeal for dredging

Canola oil for frying

1½ tablespoons extra-virgin olive oil

1 tablespoon lemon juice

2 bunches watercress or arugula (rocket), stemmed

BAKED STUFFED SOLE WITH SHRIMP SAUCE

6 tablespoons (3 oz/90 g) unsalted butter, plus extra for greasing

¼ cup (1½ oz/45 g) all-purpose (plain) flour

2 cups (16 fl oz/500 ml) whole milk

Sea salt and freshly ground white pepper

1 lb (500 g) spinach, stemmed and well washed but not dried

4 sole fillets, about 6 oz (185 g) each

½ lb (250 g) cooked cocktail shrimp

½ cup (4 fl oz/125 ml) chicken stock (page 111) or prepared low-sodium chicken broth

1 tablespoon tomato paste

Pinch of cayenne pepper, or to taste

Minced fresh chives for garnish

Preheat the oven to 375°F (190°C). Lightly butter a gratin dish measuring about 8 by 12 inches (20 by 30 cm).

In a saucepan over medium-low heat, melt the butter. Stir in the flour to make a roux *(right)* and cook, stirring constantly, for 2 or 3 minutes; do not let the mixture color. Gradually whisk in the milk. Raise the heat to medium and bring the mixture to a simmer, whisking frequently. Adjust the heat to maintain a low simmer and cook, whisking frequently, until thickened into a white sauce, about 10 minutes. Whisk in 1 teaspoon salt and white pepper to taste. Cover and set aside.

Place the spinach in a small stockpot, cover, and cook over medium heat until wilted, about 3 minutes. Empty into a colander and run cold water over to cool. In small handfuls, squeeze as much water from the spinach as possible. Using a chef's knife, chop the spinach finely. Transfer to a bowl and stir in ½ cup (4 fl oz/125 ml) of the white sauce. Season with salt and pepper to taste.

Lay out the 4 sole fillets on a cutting board, smooth skin side down, and check them for bones, removing and discarding any you find. Spoon one-fourth of the spinach mixture onto the center of each fillet, and fold the 2 ends of the fillet over the top of the spinach. Using a metal spatula, transfer each fillet to the prepared dish, seam side down.

In a blender, combine all but ¼ cup (2 oz/60 g) of the shrimp, the remaining white sauce, the stock, and the tomato paste. Purée until smooth. Transfer to a bowl and add salt and cayenne to taste.

Pour the sauce over the fish and bake until the fish is opaque throughout, about 25 minutes. Sprinkle the remaining shrimp on top of the fish and bake for 5 minutes longer. Sprinkle with the chives and serve immediately.

MAKES 4 MAIN-COURSE SERVINGS

MAKING A ROUX

A roux is a mixture of melted butter or oil and flour that is stirred over medium-low heat and used to thicken mixtures. Liquid is gradually whisked into the roux, and the mixture is cooked until thickened. A roux is a building block of such classic French sauces as béchamel and velouté, and it can be used to thicken soups and dessert sauces as well. In most cases, a roux is cooked for just 2–3 minutes to cook off the raw flour taste, and is not allowed to color, but roux used in Cajun and Creole gumbos is cooked to a range of colors, from golden to dark brown, in order to add depth of flavor.

POACHED SALMON WITH DILL SAUCE

POACHING FISH

One of the easiest and best ways to cook fish is to poach it in court bouillon, water flavored with wine or lemon juice and some herbs and vegetables. The liquid imparts flavor to whatever is poached in it. (If you are in a rush, plain water can be used as well.) Whether you are using court bouillon or water, make sure that the liquid covers the fish, and cook the fish at a bare simmer so that it will emerge at its most tender. A small roasting pan or large frying pan can be used to poach fillets, but a fish poacher is almost essential for poaching a whole fish.

Measure the salmon fillet at its thickest point. Fill a small, flame-proof roasting pan or large frying pan with 2 inches (5 cm) of water. Add the vermouth, ¼ cup lemon juice, shallots, carrot, celery, bay leaf, parsley, and 1 teaspoon salt. Bring to a boil over medium-high heat. Reduce the heat to a low simmer and place the fillet in the pan. The liquid should cover the fillet by at least 1 inch (2.5 cm); add more water if necessary. Adjust the heat so that just a few slow bubbles emerge from under the fish. Poach the fish for 10 minutes per inch of thickness; the flesh should still be translucent in the center. Using a long offset metal spatula or 2 slotted metal spatulas, transfer the fish to a platter and let cool completely. Drain off the accumulated liquid.

While the fish poaches, make the dill sauce: In a small bowl, combine the crème fraîche, yogurt, lemon juice to taste, dill, and salt and white pepper to taste. Stir to blend. Cover and refrigerate until ready to serve.

To serve, use a mandoline or a sharp knife to cut the cucumber into paper-thin slices. Beginning at the thicker end of the fish, place the cucumber slices in overlapping rows to resemble fish scales. Surround the fish with the dill sprigs, and group the lemon wedges in clusters around the fish. Serve the fish cold or at room temperature, accompanied with the dill sauce.

Serving Tip: This dish can be prepared 1 day ahead of time and refrigerated.

MAKES 6–8 MAIN-COURSE SERVINGS

1 salmon fillet, 3 lb (1.5 kg), pin bones removed

½ cup (4 fl oz/125 ml) dry white vermouth or wine

¼ cup (2 fl oz/60 ml) fresh lemon juice

2 shallots, sliced

1 small carrot, peeled and cut into 1-inch (2.5-cm) slices

1 stalk celery, cut into 1-inch (2.5-cm) slices

½ bay leaf

2 fresh flat-leaf (Italian) parsley sprigs

Sea salt

FOR THE DILL SAUCE:

½ cup (4 fl oz/125 ml) crème fraîche or sour cream

½ cup (4 oz/125 g) plain yogurt

2–3 teaspoons lemon juice

2 tablespoons minced fresh dill

Sea salt and white pepper

1 English (hothouse) cucumber

Fresh dill sprigs and lemon wedges for garnish

LOBSTER THERMIDOR

1 lb (500 g) cooked lobster meat *(far right),* including 4 whole claws if available

9 tablespoons (4½ oz/ 140 g) unsalted butter

2 green (spring) onions, including tender green parts, finely chopped

¼ cup (2 fl oz/60 ml) brandy

2 teaspoons minced fresh thyme or ½ teaspoon dried

Salt and freshly ground white pepper

½ lb (250 g) white button mushrooms, brushed clean and thinly sliced

1½ tablespoons fresh lemon juice, or to taste

3 tablespoons all-purpose (plain) flour

1½ cups (12 fl oz/375 ml) lobster stock, shrimp stock, fish stock, or chicken stock (page 111), or prepared low-sodium chicken broth

½ cup (4 fl oz/125 ml) half-and-half (half cream)

½ teaspoon sweet paprika

2–3 dashes Tabasco sauce

½ cup (2 oz/60 g) grated Parmesan cheese

Preheat the oven to 425°F (220°C). If you have whole claws, remove the meat whole (page 106) and reserve for garnishing. Cut the lobster meat into ½-inch (12-mm) dice and set aside.

In a saucepan over medium heat, melt 4 tablespoons of the butter. Add the green onions and sauté until the white part is translucent, about 3 minutes. Stir in the diced lobster and sauté until heated through, about 3 minutes. Add the brandy, bring to a simmer, and cook for 1 minute. Stir in the thyme and salt and pepper to taste. Remove from the heat and set aside.

In a nonreactive frying pan over medium heat, melt 1 tablespoon of the butter. Add the mushrooms and sauté until golden, about 5 minutes. Stir in 1 tablespoon of the lemon juice. Remove from the heat and set aside.

In a nonreactive saucepan over medium-low heat, melt the remaining 4 tablespoons butter. Stir in the flour to make a roux (see page 17) and cook, stirring constantly, for 2–3 minutes; do not let the mixture color. Gradually whisk in the stock. Cook, stirring frequently, until thickened, about 10 minutes. Stir in the half-and-half and cook, stirring frequently, for 5 minutes longer. Stir in the paprika, salt to taste, Tabasco sauce to taste, and the remaining ½ tablespoon lemon juice, or more to taste. Taste and adjust the seasoning.

Stir the lobster mixture and mushrooms into the white sauce. Spoon the lobster mixture into 4 individual gratin dishes (about 6 inches/15 cm in diameter). Sprinkle each with one-fourth of the Parmesan. Place the dishes on a baking sheet and bake until bubbling and lightly browned, about 20 minutes. Serve at once, garnished with the claw meat, if available.

MAKES 4 MAIN-COURSE SERVINGS

LOBSTER THERMIDOR
This rich dish, a lobster-and-cream mixture—classically baked and presented in the lobster shells—was created in nineteenth-century Paris to celebrate the opening of a play named *Thermidor* (after one of the months in the calendar of the French Revolution). For this recipe, purchase cooked lobster meat from a good fishmonger, or cook 4 live lobsters according to the directions in the method for Boiled Maine Lobster with Two Drawn Butters (page 102) and remove the meat from the shells as directed on page 106.

SEAFOOD PAELLA

In a frying pan over medium heat, heat 1 tablespoon of the olive oil. Add the squid tentacles and sauté them until they stiffen, 1–2 minutes. Transfer them to a plate and set aside for garnish.

To peel and seed the tomatoes, cut a shallow X in the bottom of each tomato. Bring a medium saucepan three-fourths full of water to a boil. Immerse the tomatoes for about 1 minute; transfer them to a bowl of cold water to cool for about 15 seconds. Peel off the skins and cut the tomatoes in half crosswise. Lightly squeeze and shake the tomatoes to release the seeds. Chop the tomatoes, discarding the core, and set aside.

Bring a medium saucepan of water to a boil and blanch the peas for 1 minute. Drain and transfer to a bowl of cold water to cool for about 15 seconds. Drain again and set aside.

Line the bottom of a broiler (grill) pan with aluminum foil. Preheat the broiler. Cut the bell pepper in half lengthwise; remove the stem, ribs, and seeds. Place the pepper halves, cut side down, on the prepared broiler pan and press them flat. Place the pan under the broiler about 2 inches (5 cm) from the heat source. Broil, turning occasionally, until evenly blackened on all sides, 5–8 minutes. Using tongs, transfer to a paper bag, close the bag, and let cool to the touch, about 10 minutes. Peel off the charred skin, using a paring knife to remove any stubborn bits, and cut the pepper lengthwise into narrow strips. Set aside.

Preheat the oven to 375°F (190°C). In a 15-inch (38-cm) paella pan or a 12-inch (30-cm) ovenproof sauté pan over medium-low heat, heat the remaining 4 tablespoons (2 fl oz/60 ml) olive oil. Add the onion and sauté, stirring frequently, until it softens and becomes golden, about 8 minutes. Add the garlic and cook until fragrant, about 1 minute. Add the tomatoes and cook, stirring frequently, until they soften, about 5 minutes. Add the rice and stir until well coated, 2–3 minutes.

PAELLA PANS

The classic wide, shallow metal paella pan was designed for cooking paella over an open fire; the large surface area helps the rice cook quickly and evenly. The first paellas are thought to have been made in clay casseroles. Paella made in a relatively deep casserole will yield a wetter rice, while paella made in a shallow paella pan will cook slightly faster and yield drier rice. When using a paella pan or other large, shallow pan on a stove-top burner, which will be smaller than the bottom of the vessel, you will need to place it off center and turn it periodically to cook the rice evenly.

5 tablespoons (3 fl oz/80 ml) extra-virgin olive oil

½ lb (250 g) squid, cleaned and cut into rings, tentacles reserved (page 109)

2 tomatoes

6 oz (185 g) sugar snap peas, trimmed, or 1 cup (5 oz/155 g) fresh or thawed frozen English peas

1 red bell pepper (capsicum)

1 white onion, finely chopped

2 large cloves garlic, minced

1½ cups Spanish paella rice or Arborio rice

4 cups (32 fl oz/1 l) fish stock (page 111), or 2 cups (16 fl oz/500 ml) *each* bottled clam juice and chicken stock (page 111) or prepared low-sodium chicken broth

Large pinch of saffron threads, toasted and ground (page 36)

¼ teaspoon *pimentón picante* (page 31) or sweet Hungarian paprika

½ cup (4 fl oz/125 ml) dry white vermouth or wine

Sea salt and freshly
ground black pepper

½ tablespoon fresh
lemon juice

12 large sea scallops,
trimmed if needed
(page 108)

12 black mussels, rinsed
and debearded (page 13)

12 littleneck or Manila
clams, rinsed

12 jumbo shrimp (prawns)
in the shell

Minced fresh flat-leaf
(Italian) parsley for garnish

Lemon wedges for serving

Meanwhile, bring the stock to a boil and stir in the saffron and *pimentón*. Stir the stock, vermouth, and salt and black pepper to taste into the rice. Raise the heat to medium-high and boil for 5 minutes. Stir in the lemon juice. Reduce the heat to a simmer and position the pan slightly off center on the burner. Cook until the rice has absorbed most of the liquid, about 10 minutes, smoothing the top with a large wooden spoon and turning the pan a little every few minutes so that the rice around the edges of the pan cooks evenly. Keep the pan off center on the burner, and do not stir the rice (this ensures that the rice cooks evenly and doesn't turn gummy).

For a traditional, composed arrangement of ingredients atop the paella, tuck the sliced squid into the center of the rice and press it down with a spoon. Tuck the scallops around the edge. Alternately tuck the mussels and clams into the rice, hinge side down, discarding any that do not close to the touch. Press the peas partly down into the rice among the mussels and clams. Lay the shrimp in between all the other seafood. Place the strips of bell pepper in a sunburst pattern over the top. Alternatively, intersperse the ingredients in a casual arrangement atop the rice.

Transfer the pan to the oven and bake the paella until the rice is almost al dente, about 10 minutes. Remove from the oven, cover with a clean kitchen towel, and let stand for 10 minutes. Remove and discard any mussels or clams that do not open. Garnish with the parsley and squid tentacles and serve with the lemon wedges.

MAKES 6 MAIN-COURSE SERVINGS

(Photograph appears on following page.)

RICE FOR PAELLA

Medium-grain, high-starch white rices are grown in Spain specifically for use in paella. Bomba is one popular variety. Paella rice is available in specialty-food stores and Spanish import stores, but more widely available Arborio rice is virtually identical and makes a perfect substitute. When this type of rice is used in risotto, it is stirred to release its starches and give the dish a creamy texture. In making paella, on the other hand, the goal is to produce firm yet tender separate grains, so it is important not to stir the rice once it has been thoroughly coated with oil.

QUICK DINNERS

Because fish and shellfish cook quickly and require only a few simple ingredients to bring out their flavors, they are a boon to the busy cook. The seafood dishes in this chapter, from soft-shell crab sandwiches to Cajun-spiced catfish, all go together quickly and use commonly available ingredients, making them ideal for a fast weekday meal or even an impromptu dinner party.

STIR-FRIED SHRIMP AND ASPARAGUS

STIR-FRYING SAVVY

A Chinese wok is best for stir-frying, but a sauté pan or deep frying pan may be used. Heat the pan before adding the oil, and continue to heat until the oil is almost smoking. Swirl to coat the sides as well as the bottom. Add quick-cooking foods, such as small pieces of meat, fish, or tofu, and stir constantly while they cook; transfer them to a bowl before adding slower-cooking foods, such as dense vegetables. Liquid is usually added to the pan and the pan is covered for a few minutes to cook the slower-cooking foods. Then the seafood, meat, or tofu is returned to the pan and briefly reheated.

Place the shrimp in a glass or ceramic bowl and add the salt, sesame oil, and soy sauce. Toss to coat. Cut the asparagus on the diagonal into pieces about 2 inches (5 cm) long.

In a large wok or sauté pan over medium-high heat, heat the peanut oil until the oil shimmers. Swirl the pan to coat evenly with the oil. Add the garlic, ginger, and shrimp and toss and stir until the shrimp are evenly pink on both sides, about 1 minute. Using a slotted spoon or a skimmer, transfer the shrimp to a bowl.

Add the asparagus to the pan and toss and stir over medium-high heat until bright green, about 1 minute. Add the green onion and wine. Cover the pan and cook until the asparagus is tender-crisp, about 2 minutes. Return the shrimp to the pan and toss and stir just until heated through, about 1 minute. Pour into a shallow bowl and garnish with cilantro leaves. Serve immediately, with the steamed rice.

Variation Tip: Replace the asparagus with ½ lb (250 g) snow peas, trimmed.

MAKES 4 MAIN-COURSE SERVINGS

2 lb (1 kg) large shrimp (prawns), shelled, with tail segments intact, and deveined (page 86)

1 teaspoon sea salt

1 teaspoon Asian sesame oil

1 tablespoon tamari or light soy sauce

1 bunch asparagus, ends trimmed and stalks peeled if stalks are thick and woody

2 tablespoons peanut or canola oil

2 cloves garlic, minced

1 tablespoon peeled and minced fresh ginger

1 green (spring) onion, including tender green parts, cut on the diagonal into 1-inch (2.5-cm) pieces

2 tablespoons Chinese rice wine or dry sherry

Fresh cilantro (fresh coriander) leaves for garnish

Steamed white rice for serving (page 111)

GARLIC SHRIMP

¾ cup (6 fl oz / 180 ml) extra-virgin olive oil

3–4 cloves garlic, minced

2 or 3 small dried red chiles, or red pepper flakes to taste

24 large shrimp (prawns), shelled, with tail segments intact, and deveined (see page 86)

Juice of 1 lemon

Sea salt

Pimentón picante (far right) or hot or sweet Hungarian paprika

Thick slices of coarse country bread or steamed white rice (page 111) for serving

Place 6 or 4 shallow ramekins, preferably earthenware and about 5 inches (13 cm) in diameter, in a cold oven. Adjust the heat to 400°F (200°C) and heat the ramekins for at least 20 minutes.

In a large nonreactive frying pan, combine the olive oil, garlic, and chiles. Place over medium heat until the garlic begins to turn golden, about 2 minutes. Add the shrimp and sauté until evenly pink on both sides, 2–3 minutes. Immediately remove from the heat and add the lemon juice. Sprinkle with salt and pimentón to taste. Toss quickly and immediately divide the shrimp and the flavored oil among the heated ramekins. Serve immediately, while the shrimp are still sizzling. For a first course, accompany with the bread for dipping into the oil; for a main course, serve with rice.

MAKES 6 FIRST-COURSE OR 4 MAIN-COURSE SERVINGS

PIMENTÓN AND PAPRIKA

Pimentón is a Spanish paprika made from smoked paprika chiles. Like Hungarian paprika, it comes in both hot *(picante)* and sweet varieties. Sweet Spanish *pimentón picante* adds a hint of smoke and more heat to foods than other paprika; look for it at gourmet markets and Spanish food purveyors. Hungarian paprika is widely available in supermarkets, and the sweet version may be used here for a milder dish.

GREEK SHRIMP WITH TOMATOES AND FETA CHEESE

FETA CHEESE

Feta cheese, a white, crumbly sheep's or cow's milk cheese that is pickled in brine, is made in many countries, including the United States and France, but many feta lovers are especially loyal to the original Greek and Bulgarian feta. The flavors and textures of fetas vary somewhat; Bulgarian feta is usually creamier and less salty than Greek feta. Both melt beautifully. Seek out dried Greek oregano to use in recipes with your feta; it has a more intense flavor than regular oregano.

In a large, nonreactive, flameproof casserole or sauté pan over medium heat, heat the olive oil. Add the shallots and sauté until translucent, about 3 minutes. Add the garlic and sauté until fragrant, about 1 minute. Add the wine and tomatoes (but not their juice). Add the oregano now, if using dried. Season to taste with salt, red pepper flakes, and paprika. Bring to a boil over high heat, then reduce the heat to medium and cook, stirring often, until the tomatoes begin to soften, about 5 minutes. Add some of the reserved tomato juice if you prefer a thinner sauce.

Stir in the cheese, then the shrimp. Cover the pan, reduce the heat to low, and cook until the shrimp are evenly pink and the cheese is beginning to melt, about 3 minutes. Sprinkle with the oregano, if using fresh, and the minced mint. Garnish with the mint sprigs, if using, and serve immediately from the pan.

Serving Tip: Serve with thick slices of French or Italian country-style bread for sopping up the juices.

MAKES 4 MAIN-COURSE SERVINGS

4 tablespoons (2 fl oz/60 ml) extra-virgin olive oil

2 shallots, minced

2 cloves garlic, minced

½ cup (4 fl oz/125 ml) dry white vermouth or wine

6 plum (Roma) tomatoes, chopped and juice reserved, or 1 can (14½ oz/455 g) tomatoes, drained and finely chopped, juice reserved

1 tablespoon dried Greek oregano, crumbled, or 2 tablespoons minced fresh oregano

Sea salt

Red pepper flakes

Sweet Hungarian paprika

⅔ cup (3 oz/90 g) coarsely crumbled feta cheese, preferably Greek or Bulgarian

2 lb (1 kg) large shrimp (prawns), shelled, with tail segments intact, and deveined (page 86)

2 tablespoons minced fresh mint, plus mint sprigs for garnish (optional)

PANFRIED RAINBOW TROUT
WITH BACON AND SAGE

4 whole rainbow trout, cleaned, with or without heads, ½–¾ lb (250–375 g) each

½ cup (2½ oz/75 g) stone-ground cornmeal

Sea salt

Cayenne pepper

4 large fresh sage sprigs, plus leaves from 4 sprigs

1 strip apple wood–smoked bacon

3 tablespoons extra-virgin olive oil

4 tablespoons (2 oz/60 g) unsalted butter

Juice of 1 lemon

Rinse the trout inside and out under cold running water and pat dry inside and out with paper towels. In a large, shallow bowl or plate, combine the cornmeal with salt and cayenne to taste. Stir to blend. Salt the cavity of each trout and place a sage sprig inside. Dredge the trout in the cornmeal mixture to coat both sides evenly.

In a large cast-iron or other heavy frying pan over medium heat, cook the bacon until crisp. Using tongs, transfer to paper towels to drain. Add the olive oil to the fat in the pan and heat until the oil shimmers. Add the trout, just two at a time if needed to avoid crowding, and cook until lightly browned on the outside and opaque throughout, 4–5 minutes on each side. Transfer the trout to a platter or plates in a low (200°F/95°C) oven.

Pour off all but 1 tablespoon of the fat in the pan and add the butter and sage leaves. Cook over medium heat until the butter is lightly browned and the sage leaves are crisp, about 2 minutes. Add the lemon juice and heat for about 30 seconds. Pour the mixture over the trout. Crumble the bacon strip and sprinkle one-fourth over each trout. Serve immediately.

MAKES 4 MAIN-COURSE SERVINGS

PANFRYING

Panfrying, similar to sautéing, is one of the quickest ways to cook whole fish or fillets. To panfry, start with a hot pan and heat either butter and oil or oil alone until the butter stops foaming or the oil shimmers. (Using both butter and oil gives you the good flavor of butter but makes it less likely to burn.) The food to be panfried is usually dredged in flour, cornmeal, or bread crumbs to form a crisp coating, then fried well on each side until browned. Also try this method with trout and sole fillets.

BROILED ROCKFISH WITH CHARMOULA SAUCE

TOASTING SAFFRON

Toasting and grinding saffron threads helps to bring out their flavor and allows the saffron to dissolve thoroughly in hot liquid. To do so, heat a small, dry frying pan over medium heat. Add the saffron threads and toast, stirring constantly, until the saffron is fragrant, about 30 seconds. Transfer the saffron into a small mortar and grind to a fine powder with a pestle.

To make the sauce, combine the saffron mixture, garlic, parsley, fresh cilantro, lemon zest and juice, cumin, and paprika in a small bowl. Stir in the olive oil until well blended. Add the ground coriander and salt and cayenne to taste. Taste and adjust the seasoning.

Place the rockfish fillets in a glass or ceramic dish just large enough to hold them. Spread about 1 tablespoon of the sauce over the top of each fillet. Turn and spread another 1 tablespoon sauce on the other side of each fillet. Let the fillets stand at room temperature for 30 minutes.

Preheat the broiler (grill). Line the bottom of a broiler pan with aluminum foil and oil the top with a paper towel soaked with oil. Place the fillets on the prepared pan and place the pan under the broiler 2–3 inches (5–7.5 cm) from the heat source. Broil, turning once, until lightly browned and opaque throughout, about 2 minutes on each side.

Transfer the fillets to a warmed platter or individual plates and top each with another spoonful of the sauce. Garnish liberally with the herb sprigs and serve immediately, with the remaining sauce alongside.

Note: Also spelled chermoula, charmoula *is a classic Moroccan sauce, traditionally served with fish. It has many variations: sometimes it contains tomatoes, but it almost always contains garlic, cumin, paprika, and cilantro. Colorful, fresh, and flavorful,* charmoula *is perfect on grilled or broiled, baked, or fried fish.*

MAKES 4–6 MAIN-COURSE SERVINGS

FOR THE CHARMOULA SAUCE:

Pinch of saffron threads, toasted, ground *(far left)*, and dissolved in 1 tablespoon hot water

2 cloves garlic, minced

½ cup (¾ oz/20 g) minced fresh flat-leaf (Italian) parsley

½ cup (¾ oz/20 g) minced fresh cilantro (fresh coriander)

Grated zest and juice of 1 lemon

1 teaspoon ground cumin

1 teaspoon sweet Hungarian paprika

½ cup (4 fl oz/125 ml) extra-virgin olive oil

Pinch of ground coriander

Sea salt

Cayenne pepper

4–6 rockfish fillets, 6–8 oz (185–250 g) each

Fresh flat-leaf (Italian) parsley sprigs and/or cilantro (fresh coriander) sprigs for garnish

CAJUN-SPICED CATFISH ON WILTED GREENS

FOR THE CAJUN SPICE RUB:

1 teaspoon sea salt

1 teaspoon freshly ground black pepper

½ teaspoon cayenne pepper

1 tablespoon sweet Hungarian paprika

1 teaspoon fennel seeds, toasted (page 46) and ground

1 teaspoon dried thyme, crumbled

4 catfish fillets, 6–8 oz (185–250 g) each

5 tablespoons (3 fl oz/80 ml) extra-virgin olive oil, plus extra for coating

1 strip apple wood–smoked bacon, finely diced

8 handfuls baby spinach leaves, baby arugula (rocket) leaves, or watercress leaves, or a mixture

2 cloves garlic, minced

1 tablespoon red wine vinegar

½–1 tablespoon fresh lemon juice

Sea salt and freshly ground black pepper

To make the spice rub, in a small bowl, combine the salt, black pepper, cayenne, paprika, fennel seeds, and thyme.

Place the catfish fillets in a glass or ceramic dish just large enough to hold them and coat them on both sides with olive oil. Spread a scant teaspoonful of the Cajun spice rub on each side of each fillet, coating the fillets evenly. Let stand at room temperature for 30 minutes.

Coat a large, heavy, ovenproof frying pan with olive oil and heat over medium-high heat until the oil shimmers. Add the catfish and cook until opaque throughout, about 2 minutes on each side. Transfer the pan to a low (200°F/95°C) oven to keep the fish warm.

In a separate heavy, nonreactive frying pan over medium heat, cook the bacon until crisp. Using a slotted spoon, transfer the bacon to paper towels to drain. Place the greens in a large bowl. Add the 5 tablespoons olive oil to the pan with the bacon fat and heat until the surface shimmers. Add the garlic and sauté until barely golden, about 1 minute. Remove the pan from the heat. Immediately add the vinegar and ½ tablespoon lemon juice, stir, and pour over the greens in the bowl. Toss well to wilt the greens slightly. Season with salt and black pepper to taste and, if desired, additional lemon juice.

Quickly divide the greens among 4 warmed plates, top each with a catfish fillet, and sprinkle with one-fourth of the cooked bacon. Serve immediately.

MAKES 4 MAIN-COURSE SERVINGS

SPICE RUBS

Spice rubs are a quick way to add flavor to a variety of foods, from fish to pork. They have the virtue of adding not only taste, but also a lightly crisp and colorful coating, especially in the case of panfried fish. This rub adds contrasting color and a spicy taste to mild white catfish. The salt in the rub helps the spices to penetrate the flesh of the fish and imbue it with flavor.

SOFT-SHELL CRAB SANDWICHES

SOFT-SHELL CRABS

Soft-shell crabs are blue crabs that have just molted and are therefore edible, soft shell and all. Although they are available cleaned and frozen year-round, their fresh season runs from May through August only. Because of their seasonal nature, their delectable taste, and their ease of preparation, they are beloved by East Coast cooks.

Panfrying them to make sandwiches is one of the simplest cooking methods, and one that evokes the feeling of summer for crab lovers in coastal areas.

To make the aioli, using a large mortar or small bowl and a pestle, grind the garlic and a pinch of salt together. Add the egg yolk and whisk until thick and sticky, about 15 seconds. Gradually whisk in the canola oil a drop at a time until the sauce thickens. Whisk in the remaining canola oil in a fine stream, then whisk in the olive oil. Whisk in the *harissa*, hot water, and lemon juice. Add salt and white pepper to taste and more *harissa*, if you like.

Plunge the crabs into a large stockpot of boiling salted water, cover the pot, reduce the heat to medium-high, and cook for 1 minute. Using tongs, transfer the crabs to a work surface.

To clean the crabs, use kitchen scissors to cut off the eyes and mouth parts. Pull up the pointed end of the shell and scrape out the spongy matter underneath. Turn the crabs on their backs and cut off their tails and the gills on each side. Rinse under cold water and pat dry with paper towels. Place the flour and the egg mixture in separate shallow bowls. Put the cornmeal in a third shallow bowl and season to taste with salt and paprika.

In a large, heavy sauté pan over medium-high heat, heat ½ inch (12 mm) of olive oil until the oil shimmers. Dredge the crabs first in the flour, then in the egg mixture, and then in the cornmeal mixture. Fry the crabs, two at a time if needed to avoid crowding, until browned all over and crisp on the edges, 3–4 minutes. Meanwhile, toast the focaccia.

To make the sandwiches, spread the toasted bread with the aioli and layer with the just-cooked crabs and watercress. Serve at once.

Notes: A fiery chile sauce from the Middle East, harissa *is available in jars and tubes. If you can't find it, substitute Tabasco sauce. The aioli in this recipe includes raw egg; see page 113 for more information.*

MAKES 4 MAIN-COURSE SERVINGS

FOR THE SPICY AIOLI:

1 clove garlic, minced

Sea salt and freshly ground white pepper

1 egg yolk (see Notes)

⅓ cup (3 fl oz/80 ml) canola oil

2 tablespoons extra-virgin olive oil

1 teaspoon *harissa*, or to taste (see Notes), or ¼–½ teaspoon Tabasco sauce

1 tablespoon hot water

½ tablespoon fresh lemon juice, or to taste

4 live soft-shell crabs

1 cup (5 oz/155 g) all-purpose (plain) flour

1 egg beaten with 2 tablespoons water

1 cup (5 oz/155 g) cornmeal

Sea salt

Sweet or hot Hungarian paprika

Olive oil for frying

4 pieces focaccia bread, halved horizontally

Watercress or arugula (rocket) leaves for serving

CLAMS WITH ANGEL HAIR PASTA

Sea salt and freshly
ground white pepper

4 tablespoons (2 fl oz/60 ml)
extra-virgin olive oil

2 cloves garlic, minced

Red pepper flakes

6 plum (Roma) tomatoes,
finely diced and juice
reserved, or 1 can (14½ oz/
455 g) tomatoes, drained
and finely diced, juice
reserved

1 cup (8 fl oz/250 ml) dry
white vermouth or wine

24 littleneck or Manila
clams, rinsed

¾ lb (375 g) capellini
(angel hair) pasta

2 tablespoons minced
fresh flat-leaf (Italian)
parsley

2 tablespoons minced
fresh mint

Bring a large pot of water to a boil and add a generous amount of salt.

Meanwhile, in a large, nonreactive sauté pan over medium heat, heat the olive oil. Add the garlic and red pepper flakes to taste and sauté until fragrant, about 1 minute. Add the tomatoes and their juice, the wine, and salt and pepper to taste. Sauté until the tomatoes begin to soften, 2–3 minutes. Add the clams, discarding any that do not close to the touch, cover, and cook until the clams open, 4–5 minutes. Check once or twice during the cooking time and transfer the clams that have already opened to a bowl. Discard any clams that do not open.

When the clams are halfway though cooking, add the pasta to the boiling water and cook until al dente, about 2 minutes. Drain the pasta, reserving a little of the pasta water. When all of the clams are cooked and have been transferred to the bowl, add the pasta to the sauté pan and stir to coat with the sauce. Add a little of the pasta water if needed to thin the sauce enough to coat the pasta lightly. Return the clams to the pan along with any accumulated juices. Sprinkle the pasta with salt and white pepper to taste, then sprinkle with the parsley and mint. Toss lightly. Serve immediately in a large warmed pasta bowl or individual shallow bowls.

MAKES 4 MAIN-COURSE SERVINGS

PASTA TIPS

Use a large pot of water to
cook the pasta quickly and
evenly, and add a generous
amount of salt to the water
after it reaches a boil to replace
the salt leached from the pasta
as it cooks. Always stir dried
pasta immediately after adding
it to the water and once or
twice during cooking to keep
it from sticking together. Cook
until al dente, tender but still
chewy. When draining pasta,
reserve a little of the cooking
water to add to the sauce if
necessary; its starch content
will thicken a sauce slightly.
Use cooked pasta right away.
If it must sit, toss it lightly with
olive oil to prevent sticking.

SEAFOOD IN THE OVEN

Baking, roasting, and broiling are almost foolproof methods of fish cookery, and an amazing variety of dishes can be prepared in these ways. Some of the recipes in this chapter, such as the roasted mussels, take only minutes to prepare, while others, like the roast lobster, are more elaborate. In every case, the dry heat of the oven brings out the best of the seafood's flavor.

PAN-ROASTED MUSSELS WITH FENNEL SEEDS, SAFFRON, AND BASIL

Preheat the oven to 400°F (200°C).

In a large cast-iron frying pan or ovenproof sauté pan over medium heat, melt the butter with the olive oil until the butter foams. Add the garlic and red pepper flakes to taste and sauté until fragrant, about 1 minute. Add the mussels, discarding any that do not close to the touch, the fennel seeds, the saffron mixture, and the wine. Raise the heat to high and sauté for about 30 seconds. Transfer the pan to the oven and roast until the mussels open, 4–6 minutes.

Remove the pan from the oven. Remove and discard any mussels that have not opened. Sprinkle the mussels with the basil and salt to taste. Serve immediately, in the pan.

Serving Tip: Accompany with thick slices of French or Italian country-style bread, grilled or toasted and brushed on one side with olive oil.

MAKES 4 MAIN-COURSE SERVINGS

TOASTING SEEDS AND NUTS

To toast seeds, heat a small, dry frying pan over medium heat. Add the seeds and sauté, stirring constantly, until they are lightly toasted and fragrant, 30–60 seconds. Pour into a bowl to cool. Nuts can be toasted in the same way, but since they must cook for several minutes, they are liable to burn if not watched carefully and stirred or tossed often. A safer method is to spread the nuts on a baking sheet and toast them in a preheated 375°F (190°C) oven for 5–8 minutes, depending on size; stir them once halfway through.

2 tablespoons unsalted butter

2 tablespoons extra-virgin olive oil

4 cloves garlic, minced

Red pepper flakes

2 lb (1 kg) large black mussels, rinsed and debearded (page 13)

1 teaspoon fennel seeds, toasted *(far left)*

Pinch of saffron threads, toasted, ground (page 36), and dissolved in 1 table-spoon hot water

½ cup (4 fl oz/125 ml) dry white vermouth or wine

⅓ cup (½ oz/15 g) finely shredded fresh basil leaves

Sea salt

ROAST LOBSTER WITH TARRAGON BUTTER

4 live Maine lobsters,
1¼–1½ lb (625–750 g) each

¼ cup (2 oz/60 g) kosher
salt

Tarragon Butter *(far right)*

Lemon wedges for garnish

Fresh tarragon sprigs
for garnish

Fill a large stockpot with enough water to cover the lobsters and bring to a boil over high heat. Add the salt. Remove the lobsters from the refrigerator; leave any rubber bands on the claws. (If the pot will hold only 2 lobsters, remove them from the refrigerator 2 at a time.) Plunge the lobsters, head down, into the water. Cover the pot and listen carefully to determine when the water returns to a full boil; this could take 5 or 6 minutes. Leaving the pot covered, cook the lobsters for 5 minutes from the time the water returns to a boil; they will be half-cooked.

Using tongs, remove the lobsters from the pot and rinse under cold running water for a few seconds. Remove any rubber bands from the claws. To drain, plunge a knife into the head of each lobster, between the eyes, and hold the lobster over the sink, holding it up first by the tail, then by the claws, and then by the tail again.

Turn each lobster on its back. If desired, remove the smaller legs. Using a chef's knife, cut each lobster in half vertically, head to tail. Holding the tails at each end, bend the tails to crack them so that they will lie flat. Using a spoon, remove and discard the greenish sacs just below the heads. Remove and discard the intestinal tracts that run along the bottom of the shells from head to tail. Insert a long wooden skewer on one side of the large end of each lobster tail and push it to extend all the way through the tail to keep it flat while roasting. If desired, leave the tomalley and any roe.

Arrange 2 oven racks in the upper third and the center of the oven. Preheat to 425°F (220°C). Place 4 lobster halves, cut side up and facing opposite directions, on each of 2 baking sheets. Spread one-eighth of the tarragon butter over the cut side of each lobster half. Place the baking sheets in the oven and roast the lobster until the meat is opaque, about 5 minutes. Serve on large warmed plates, garnished with the lemon wedges and tarragon sprigs.

MAKES 4 MAIN-COURSE SERVINGS

TARRAGON BUTTER

Tarragon, with its sweet, faintly licorice flavor, is a classic French companion to seafood, especially lobster. It seems to bring out the incomparable sweetness of this shellfish, but it is also good with other seafood, such as scallops and sea bass. To make tarragon butter, combine ½ cup (4 oz/ 125 g) unsalted butter at room temperature; 2 shallots, minced; ¼ cup (¼ oz/7 g) fresh tarragon leaves, minced; and 1 tablespoon fresh lemon juice in a small bowl. Stir to blend. Add salt and freshly ground pepper (preferably white pepper) to taste and stir again.

BAKED SALMON WITH WATERCRESS SAUCE

Preheat the oven to 425°F (220°C).

To make the sauce, in a saucepan, melt the butter over medium-low heat. Add the shallot and sauté until translucent, about 3 minutes. Stir in the 1 tablespoon flour to make a roux (see page 17) and cook, stirring constantly, for 2–3 minutes; do not let the mixture color. Stir in the watercress and spinach until wilted. Add the stock and simmer for about 5 minutes. Stir in the cream. Transfer to a blender and purée until smooth. Return to the pan and add sea salt and white pepper to taste. Set aside and cover to keep warm.

In a shallow bowl, combine the ¼ cup flour with a generous sprinkle of salt and white pepper. Very lightly dredge the top side of the salmon fillets in the flour.

Lightly coat a large ovenproof sauté pan with olive oil and heat over medium-high heat until the oil shimmers. Add the salmon, top side down, and sear for 2 minutes. Turn the salmon over and transfer the pan to the oven. Roast the salmon for exactly 8 minutes; it should still be translucent in the center of the thickest part.

Just before the salmon is done, reheat the sauce over low heat until warm, 2–3 minutes. Transfer the salmon to warmed plates. Spoon one-fourth of the sauce onto each plate and place a fillet on top, or spoon the sauce over the center of each fillet, allowing the ends to show and the sauce to pool on the plate. Garnish each fillet with a watercress sprig and serve immediately.

MAKES 4 MAIN-COURSE SERVINGS

WATERCRESS

This peppery green, which grows in the wild in cold streams, has a natural affinity with fish. Its flavor is spicy and clean, and its rounded leaves are a vibrant green. Watercress can be used as a bed to serve fish on, as a garnish, as an ingredient in soups and sauces, or, of course, in a refreshing salad to accompany fish. Store watercress in a perforated bag in the refrigerator for up to 2 days. Remove the stems before using.

FOR THE WATERCRESS SAUCE:

2 tablespoons unsalted butter

1 shallot, minced

1 tablespoon all-purpose (plain) flour

1 bunch watercress, stemmed, 4 sprigs reserved for garnish

1 cup (1 oz/30 g) packed spinach leaves

¾ cup (6 fl oz/180 ml) chicken stock (page 111) or prepared low-sodium chicken broth

¼ cup (2 fl oz/60 ml) heavy (double) cream

Sea salt and freshly ground pepper

¼ cup (1½ oz/45 g) all-purpose (plain) flour

Sea salt and freshly ground pepper

4 salmon fillets, 6–8 oz (185–250 g) each, pin bones removed

Extra-virgin olive oil for coating

BROILED LINGCOD WITH MISO GLAZE

4 lingcod fillets, 6–8 oz (185–250 g) each, pin bones removed

2 tablespoons peanut or canola oil

1 tablespoon tamari or light soy sauce

1 tablespoon peeled and minced fresh ginger

FOR THE MISO GLAZE:

½ cup (4 oz/125 g) red miso paste

2 tablespoons dry white vermouth or wine

2 tablespoons peanut or canola oil

1 tablespoon honey

1 tablespoon fresh lemon juice

1 clove garlic, crushed through a garlic press

1½ tablespoons sesame seeds, toasted (page 46)

Fresh cilantro (fresh coriander) sprigs for garnish

Place the lingcod fillets in a small glass or ceramic dish just large enough to hold them. In a small bowl, combine the oil, tamari, and ginger. Stir to blend. Pour the mixture over the fillets and turn to coat on both sides. Let the fillets stand at room temperature for 30 minutes.

Meanwhile, make the miso glaze: In a small saucepan, combine the miso paste, vermouth, oil, honey, lemon juice, and garlic and stir to blend. Place over low heat and bring to a simmer; cook for 2–3 minutes to allow the flavors to blend, then remove from the heat and set aside.

Preheat the broiler (grill). Line the bottom of a broiler pan with aluminum foil and oil the top with a paper towel soaked with oil. Measure the lingcod fillets at their thickest point. Place the fish, rounded side down, on the prepared pan and place the pan under the broiler 2–3 inches (5–7.5 cm) from the heat source. Broil for 2 minutes. Remove the pan from the broiler, turn the fish over, and spread the miso glaze evenly over the top. Place the pan under the broiler again and cook until the fish is opaque throughout, about 3 minutes longer; the total cooking time should be about 5 minutes per ½ inch (12 mm) thickness of the fish.

Serve the fish immediately on warmed plates or a platter, sprinkled with the sesame seeds and garnished with the cilantro.

MAKES 4 MAIN-COURSE SERVINGS

MISO

This Japanese soybean paste comes in three colors: yellow (also called white), red, and dark brown; the taste intensifies as the color darkens. Look for it in the Asian section of many supermarkets and in Asian markets. It will keep indefinitely in the refrigerator after opening. In addition to using miso when cooking fish, you can use it to flavor soups and sauces.

ROAST SEA BASS ON A BED OF FENNEL

Preheat the oven to 400°F (200°C).

Quarter the fennel bulbs lengthwise and cut away the tough core portion. Coat the slices with olive oil, then sprinkle with salt and pepper to taste. Divide among 4 individual gratin dishes. Roast until almost tender, about 20 minutes.

Meanwhile, place the fish fillets in a glass or ceramic dish just large enough to hold them. Sprinkle with salt and white pepper on both sides. In a small bowl, combine the 2 tablespoons olive oil, the Pernod, garlic, lemon zest, and lemon juice. Stir to blend, then pour over the fish. Turn to coat the fish on both sides. Let stand at room temperature for about 20 minutes.

When the fennel is almost tender and the fish is marinated, remove the gratin dishes from the oven. Use a spatula to place a fillet on top of each bed of fennel. Pour the remaining marinade over the fish. Return the dishes to the oven and roast until the fish is opaque throughout and the fennel is lightly browned and tender when pierced with a knife, about 10 minutes.

Finely chop some of the reserved fennel fronds and sprinkle them over the fish. Serve at once, passing the lemon wedges at the table.

MAKES 4 MAIN-COURSE SERVINGS

FENNEL

Fennel, with its mild anise taste and crisp texture, is a classic partner for fish. Look for smooth, rounded bulbs, and cut off any discolored spots, as well as the stems and their feathery fronds. Reserve the stems for soup and the fronds for a garnish, either whole or finely chopped. Cut the fennel bulb in half or quarters length-wise and cut out the core at the base before using as called for in recipes. Adding an anise-flavored liqueur, such as Pernod from France, intensifies the fennel flavor.

3 fennel bulbs, 8–10 oz (250–315 g) each, trimmed, fronds reserved

2 tablespoons extra-virgin olive oil, plus extra for coating

Salt and freshly ground white pepper

4 blue-nose sea bass fillets, 6–8 oz (185–250 g) each

3 tablespoons Pernod or other anise-flavored liqueur

2 cloves garlic, minced

Grated zest of 1 lemon

1 tablespoon fresh lemon juice

Lemon wedges for serving

HALIBUT IN PARCHMENT WITH BASIL OIL

FOR THE BASIL OIL:

1 cup (1 oz/30 g) packed fresh basil leaves

½ cup (4 fl oz/125 ml) extra-virgin olive oil

1 tablespoon fresh lemon juice

1 clove garlic, minced

Sea salt and freshly ground white pepper

4 halibut fillets, 6–8 oz (185–250 g) each

Extra-virgin olive oil for coating

Sea salt and freshly ground white pepper

¼ cup (1 oz/30 g) pine nuts, toasted (page 46)

Preheat the oven to 375°F (190°C).

To make the basil oil, bring a pot of water to a boil. Blanch the basil in the boiling water for 30 seconds. Immediately empty the basil and water into a colander or sieve and run cold water over the basil to stop the cooking. In small handfuls, squeeze as much water from the basil as possible. In a blender, combine the basil, olive oil, lemon juice, and garlic. Purée until smooth. Season with salt and white pepper to taste. Set aside at room temperature.

Cut 4 pieces of parchment (baking) paper, each as long as the paper is wide. Fold each piece in half and use a pencil to draw a half heart, with the center at the fold, taking up the full width and length of the paper. Cut out the hearts with scissors. Place 1 paper heart, opened flat, on a work surface, with the point of the heart facing you.

Coat the fillets with olive oil and sprinkle both sides with salt and white pepper. Place a fillet in the center of one half of the parchment heart. Spoon one-fourth of the basil oil over each fillet. Fold the paper over so the edges match. Beginning at the top of the heart, at the end of the curve, fold the edges together, making small overlapping folds all the way to the bottom point of the heart. Fold the point under to prevent leakage. Repeat with the remaining fillets and parchment hearts.

Place the packets on a baking sheet and bake for 10 minutes. Transfer each packet to a warmed dinner plate and cut an X in the top with scissors (be careful of the escaping hot steam). Sprinkle each fillet with 1 tablespoon of the toasted nuts. Serve at once.

MAKES 4 MAIN-COURSE SERVINGS

COOKING IN PARCHMENT

Baking fish in parchment paper, a quick cooking method, gently preserves the fish's tenderness while capturing its flavor. The fish may be placed on a bed of herbs or vegetables, or topped with a sauce, flavored oil, or butter. Cooking fish inside a packet intensifies its taste and envelops the fish with a cloud of fragrance that is released when the parchment is cut for serving.

SUMMER GRILLING

Fish and shellfish are ideal for grilling. In only a few minutes, they are cooked until crisp and grill marked on the outside, tender within, and imbued with the flavors of the seasonings and smoke. Best of all, in the time it takes for the coals to reach the right temperature, you can briefly marinate fish or shellfish or prepare a sauce that perfectly complements the seafood.

GRILLED AHI TUNA WITH MANGO SALSA

Prepare a charcoal or gas grill for grilling over high heat. You may also use a broiler (grill); line the bottom of a broiler pan with aluminum foil.

Place the tuna steaks in a glass or ceramic dish just large enough to hold them. In a small bowl, whisk together the oil, lime juice, and sea salt and white pepper to taste. Pour the mixture over the steaks and turn to coat them on both sides. Let stand at room temperature for 30 minutes.

Meanwhile, make the salsa. In a small bowl, combine the diced mangoes, onion, chile, cilantro, lime juice, vinegar, and ginger, if using. Taste and adjust the seasoning. Set the salsa aside at room temperature to let the flavors combine.

Preheat the broiler now, if using.

Oil the grill rack or the top of a broiler pan with an oil-soaked paper towel. Measure the thickness of the tuna steaks. Place the tuna steaks on the grill rack, or place them on the oiled broiler pan and place the pan under the broiler 2–3 inches (5–7.5 cm) from the heat source. Cook steaks ½ inch (12 mm) thick for 3 minutes on each side for medium-rare, 1–2 minutes for rare; adjust the cooking time for thicker steaks accordingly.

Transfer the steaks to warmed dinner plates and dollop the salsa alongside or on top of the steaks. Serve immediately, garnished with the lime wedges and with marinated red onions, if you like.

Note: Seeding a chile will remove a good deal of its spiciness.

MAKES 4 MAIN-COURSE SERVINGS

CUBING MANGOES

To cut a mango into cubes, stand the fruit on one of its narrow edges, with the stem end facing you. Using a large, sharp knife, slice lengthwise slightly off center, just grazing the large central pit, removing the flesh in a single piece. Repeat on the other side of the pit. One at a time, hold each piece flesh side up. With the knife tip, score the flesh lengthwise and then cross-wise, creating a lattice pattern of ¼-inch (6-mm) cubes; take care not to pierce the peel. Press against center of the peel to pop up the cubes, then slice across the bottom of the cubes to free them.

4 ahi tuna steaks, 6–8 oz (185–250 g) each

3 tablespoons peanut or canola oil, plus extra for greasing

Juice of 1 lime

Sea salt and freshly ground white pepper

FOR THE MANGO SALSA:

2 ripe mangoes, peeled, pitted, and cut into ¼-inch (6-mm) dice *(far left)*

⅓ cup (2 oz/60 g) finely diced red onion

½–1 red serrano or jalapeño chile, seeded if desired (see Note) and minced

⅓ cup (½ oz/15 g) chopped fresh cilantro (fresh coriander)

Juice of 1 lime

2 tablespoons seasoned rice vinegar

1 tablespoon peeled and minced fresh ginger (optional)

Lime wedges for garnish

Marinated red onion (page 94) for garnish (optional)

60

GRILLED RED SNAPPER WITH ROMESCO SAUCE

4 red snapper fillets,
6–8 oz (185–250 g) each

Extra-virgin olive oil for
coating

Sea salt and freshly
ground pepper

FOR THE ROMESCO SAUCE:

1 red bell pepper
(capsicum), roasted
and peeled *(far right)*

4 tablespoons (2 fl oz/60 ml)
extra-virgin olive oil

½ cup (2½ oz/75 g) raw
almonds

½ cup (1 oz/30 g) French
or Italian bread cubes,
with crust

2 cloves garlic

¼ teaspoon cayenne
pepper, or to taste

1 tablespoon fresh
lemon juice

Sea salt

Vegetable oil for greasing

Prepare a charcoal or gas grill for grilling over high heat. You may also use a broiler (grill); line the bottom of a broiler pan with aluminum foil.

Coat the snapper fillets with olive oil and sprinkle on both sides with salt and pepper. Let stand at room temperature for 30 minutes.

To make the sauce, remove the stem, seeds, and membranes from the peeled roasted pepper if not already done. (Don't worry if a little of the charred skin remains, and don't rinse the pepper, as this washes away some of the flavor.) Put the roasted pepper in a blender. In a nonreactive sauté pan, heat 1 tablespoon of the olive oil over medium heat and sauté the almonds and bread cubes until lightly browned, about 3 minutes. Add them to the blender with the bell pepper. Add the garlic, cayenne, lemon juice, ¼ teaspoon salt, and the remaining 3 tablespoons olive oil. Purée to a grainy sauce. Taste and adjust the seasoning. Transfer to a bowl and set aside.

Preheat the broiler now, if using. Oil the grill rack or the top of the broiler pan with an oil-soaked paper towel. Place the fillets on the grill rack, or place on the prepared broiler pan and place the pan under the broiler 2–3 inches (5–7.5 cm) from the heat source. Cook the fillets, turning once, until lightly browned and opaque throughout, 2–3 minutes on each side. Immediately transfer the fillets to warmed individual plates and spoon some of the *romesco* sauce on top. Pass extra sauce alongside.

Note: Vibrantly colored and deeply flavored romesco *sauce, which comes from the Spanish region of Catalonia, is good on most kinds of fish. Also try it with grilled chicken, or spread it on slices of grilled Italian bread that have been brushed with a little olive oil.*

MAKES 4 MAIN-COURSE SERVINGS

ROASTING BELL PEPPERS

Place bell peppers over a hot fire in a grill, in a hot grill pan, or on a broiler pan about 2 inches (5 cm) from the heat source and cook, turning occasionally, until evenly blackened on all sides. (If a recipe calls for the peppers to be sliced or chopped after peeling, cut the peppers in half, remove the seeds and ribs, and place the peppers, cut side down, on a broiler pan lined with foil; press flat, so they will char more evenly.) Using tongs, transfer the roasted peppers to a paper bag, seal, and let cool to the touch, about 10 minutes. Peel off the blackened skin, using a paring knife if needed.

FISH TACOS WITH SALSA CRUDA AND GUACAMOLE

Prepare a charcoal or gas grill for grilling over medium-high heat. You may also use a broiler (grill); line the bottom of a broiler pan with aluminum foil.

Place the fillets in a glass or ceramic dish just large enough to hold them. In a small bowl, combine the oil, cumin, and chile powder. Pour over the fish and turn to coat evenly on both sides. Let stand at room temperature for about 30 minutes.

Wrap the tortillas in aluminum foil. If using a grill, place the tortillas on the edge of grill rack and let them heat for about 10 minutes on each side. If using a broiler, preheat the broiler now and place the tortilla packet in the oven to heat for about 20 minutes. Meanwhile, make the salsa cruda and the guacamole.

To make the guacamole, combine the avocado, garlic, cilantro, and lime juice in a blender. Purée until smooth. Transfer to a bowl and add the Tabasco sauce and salt to taste. Cover the bowl with plastic wrap and set aside.

Oil the grill rack or the top of the broiler pan with a paper towel soaked with oil. Place the peppers and fish fillets on the grill rack, or place on the prepared broiler pan and place the pan under the broiler 2–3 inches (5–7.5 cm) from the heat source. Cook the peppers until softened and lightly browned, 4–5 minutes. Cook the fillets, turning once, until lightly browned and opaque throughout, 2–3 minutes on each side. Transfer the peppers and fish to a cutting board and cut into strips.

Place 2 tortillas on each of 4 warmed individual plates. Divide the peppers and fish evenly among the tortillas. Top the tacos with the *salsa cruda* and guacamole. Serve at once, garnished with the cilantro sprigs and lemon wedges.

MAKES 4 MAIN-COURSE SERVINGS

SALSA CRUDA

This classic Mexican salsa, whose name means "raw sauce," is a cinch to put together. To make the salsa, combine 2 tomatoes, cut into ¼-inch (6-mm) dice; ⅓ cup (2 oz/60 g) finely diced red onion; ⅓ cup (½ oz/10 g) chopped fresh cilantro (fresh coriander); ¼–½ jalapeño chile, seeded (if desired) and minced; 1 tablespoon fresh lime juice; and 1 teaspoon seasoned rice vinegar in a small bowl. Add sea salt to taste. Set aside to let the flavors marry.

4 rock cod, rockfish, or red snapper fillets, 6–8 oz (185–250 g) each

¼ cup (2 fl oz/60 ml) canola or grapeseed oil, plus extra for greasing

½ teaspoon ground cumin

½ teaspoon pure chile powder

8 corn tortillas

Salsa Cruda *(far left)*

FOR THE GUACAMOLE:

1 ripe avocado, peeled and pitted

2 cloves garlic

¼ cup (⅓ oz/10 g) chopped fresh cilantro (fresh coriander)

2 tablespoons fresh lime juice

4 dashes Tabasco sauce, or to taste

Sea salt

1 *each* red and yellow bell peppers (capsicum), halved lengthwise and seeded

Fresh cilantro (fresh coriander) sprigs for garnish

Lime wedges for garnish

GRILLED MAHIMAHI WITH HOISIN GLAZE

FOR THE HOISIN GLAZE:

2 cloves garlic, minced

¼ cup (2 fl oz/60 ml) hoisin sauce

2 tablespoons tamari or light soy sauce

¼ cup (2 fl oz/60 ml) peanut or canola oil

2 tablespoons peeled and minced fresh ginger

2 tablespoons seasoned rice vinegar

2 or 3 dashes Asian chile oil

½ tablespoon fresh lemon juice

2 green (spring) onions, including tender green parts, finely chopped

4 mahimahi fillets, 6–8 oz (185–250 g) each

Peanut or canola oil for greasing

Fresh cilantro (fresh coriander) sprigs for garnish

Prepare a charcoal or gas grill for grilling over high heat. You may also use a broiler (grill); line the bottom of a broiler pan with aluminum foil.

To make the glaze, combine the garlic, hoisin, tamari, peanut oil, ginger, vinegar, chile oil, lemon juice, and green onions in a small bowl and stir to blend. Taste and adjust the seasoning.

Measure the mahimahi fillets at their thickest point. Place the fillets in a shallow glass or ceramic dish just large enough to hold them, pour the glaze over them, and turn to coat evenly on both sides. Let stand at room temperature for 30 minutes, turning the fillets twice.

Preheat the broiler now, if using.

Oil the grill rack or the top of the broiler pan with a paper towel soaked with oil. Using a slotted metal spatula and reserving the marinade, transfer the fillets to the grill rack, or to the broiler pan and place the pan under the broiler 2–3 inches (5–7.5 cm) from the heat source. Cook the fillets, turning once, until opaque throughout, 4–5 minutes on each side; the total time should equal about 10 minutes per inch of thickness. Transfer the fish to a platter or individual plates and keep warm in a low (200°F/95°C) oven.

While the fish is cooking, pour the reserved marinade into a small, heavy nonreactive saucepan. Bring to a boil over medium-low heat or on the edge of the grill and cook for 5 minutes. Pour the glaze evenly over the fish, garnish with the cilantro sprigs, and serve at once.

MAKES 4 MAIN-COURSE SERVINGS

HOISIN SAUCE

This spicy, slightly sweet, brownish red sauce, made with soybeans, is enlivened with five-spice powder, garlic, and dried chile. It is widely available in bottles and jars in the Asian section of most supermarkets. Once opened, it will keep indefinitely in the refrigerator. Hoisin sauce is a versatile ingredient that adds color and delicious flavor to many meat, poultry, and seafood dishes.

SEAFOOD AND VEGETABLE SKEWERS WITH HERB MARINADE

Prepare a charcoal or gas grill for grilling over medium-high heat. You may also use a broiler (grill); line the bottom of a broiler pan with aluminum foil. Soak 12 long wooden skewers in water to cover for 30 minutes; drain.

To make the marinade, combine the olive oil, basil, parsley, mint, and garlic in a glass or ceramic bowl. Add a pinch or two of red pepper flakes, the lemon juice, and salt to taste. Stir to blend. Add the shrimp, scallops, zucchini, and summer squash to the bowl. Cut the red pepper into 1-inch (2.5-cm) squares and add to the bowl. Toss to coat the shellfish and vegetables with the marinade. Let stand for about 30 minutes.

Preheat the broiler now, if using. Alternately thread 3 shrimp and 3 scallops on each of 4 skewers; thread the shrimp by going first through the thickest end, then the tail end, and thread the scallops horizontally through the sides. Alternately thread the zucchini and summer squash horizontally on the remaining 8 skewers, placing a piece of bell pepper after each squash slice (if using).

Oil the grill rack or the top of the broiler pan with a paper towel soaked with vegetable oil. Place the vegetable skewers on the grill rack, or place on the prepared broiler pan and place the pan under the broiler 2–3 inches (5–7.5 cm) from the heat source. Cook until softened and lightly grill marked, 4–5 minutes on each side. Grill or broil the seafood skewers until the scallops are opaque and and the shrimp are evenly pink, about 1½ minutes on each side.

Immediately transfer 1 seafood skewer and 2 vegetable skewers to each of 4 warmed plates. Serve immediately, accompanied with the lemon wedges.

MAKES 4 MAIN-COURSE SERVINGS

MARINATING SEAFOOD

Always marinate seafood in a ceramic or glass container, as a metal container, even a nonreactive one, can impart a metallic taste to seafood. A marinade adds flavor, and the oil in the marinade helps keep the fish or shellfish from sticking to the pan or grill. But take care when using a marinade containing citrus juice. Even a small amount of citrus will tend to "cook" the outside of the seafood, so don't use more than is specified in a recipe or marinate seafood for longer than 30 minutes at room temperature.

FOR THE HERB MARINADE:

½ cup (4 fl oz/125 ml) extra-virgin olive oil

2 tablespoons minced fresh basil

2 tablespoons minced flat-leaf (Italian) parsley

1 tablespoon minced fresh mint

2 cloves garlic, minced

Red pepper flakes

1 tablespoon fresh lemon juice

Sea salt

12 large or jumbo shrimp (prawns), shelled, with tail segments intact, and deveined (page 86)

12 large sea scallops, trimmed if needed (page 108)

1 *each* zucchini (courgette) and summer squash, cut crosswise into slices ½ inch (12 mm) thick

1 red bell pepper (capsicum), halved lengthwise and seeded (optional)

Vegetable oil for greasing

Lemon wedges for serving

GRILLED CALAMARI ON A BED OF WHITE BEANS

FOR THE WHITE BEANS:

**1 cup (7 oz/220 g)
dried cannellini or
Great Northern beans,
rinsed and picked over**

1 bay leaf

1 small dried red chile

¼ small yellow onion

1 sprig fresh thyme

**Sea salt and freshly
ground white pepper**

FOR THE VINAIGRETTE:

**4 tablespoons (2 fl oz/60 ml)
extra-virgin olive oil**

**1 tablespoon red wine
vinegar**

**Salt and freshly ground
white pepper**

**1½–2 lb (750 g–1 kg)
squid, cleaned (page 109)**

**Extra-virgin olive oil for
coating**

**Salt and freshly ground
white pepper**

**8 handfuls baby arugula
(rocket) leaves**

Salsa Verde *(far right)*

To make the beans, in a medium saucepan, combine the beans and cold water to cover by 2 inches (5 cm). Soak the beans overnight, then drain and add fresh cold water to cover by 2 inches. Alternatively, bring the beans to a boil over medium-high heat, cook for 2 minutes, then remove from the heat, cover, and let stand for 1 hour. Drain and add fresh water to cover.

Add the bay leaf, chile, onion quarter, and thyme sprig to the beans, and bring to a low boil over medium-high heat. Reduce the heat at once to a very low simmer and cook until the beans are tender, about 1 hour. Add sea salt and white pepper to taste. Set the beans in their broth aside.

Prepare a charcoal or gas grill for grilling over medium-high heat. Soak 8 long wooden skewers in water for 30 minutes, then drain.

To make the vinaigrette, whisk together the oil and vinegar in a small bowl, then whisk in salt and pepper to taste. Set aside.

Thread the squid bodies and tentacles onto the skewers. Coat with oil and sprinkle both sides with salt and pepper.

Oil the grill rack with a paper towel soaked with oil. Place the skewers on the grill rack or broil 2–3 inches (5–7.5 cm) from the heat source, turning once, until the squid is lightly colored, 1–2 minutes on each side. Transfer to a plate.

Drain the beans of almost all their broth and discard the bay leaf, chile, onion, and thyme sprig. Reheat over low heat if necessary.

Toss the beans with half of the vinaigrette. Toss the greens with the remaining vinaigrette. To serve, pile one-fourth of the greens on each plate and top with one-fourth of the beans and 2 skewers of calamari. Spoon a little of the *salsa verde* over each skewer and pass the remaining sauce at the table.

MAKES 4 MAIN-COURSE SERVINGS

SALSA VERDE

This fresh "green sauce" is delicious on nearly any grilled seafood. To make it, in a bowl, using a wooden spoon, mash together ½ cup (4 fl oz/125 ml) extra-virgin olive oil and 1 slice country-style bread, soaked in water and squeezed dry, to form a paste. Stir in 1 cup (1 oz/30 g) fresh flat-leaf (Italian) parsley leaves, minced; 2 tablespoons capers, drained and finely chopped; 4 oil-packed anchovy fillets, finely chopped; 3 garlic cloves, minced; and 1–2 teaspoons red wine vinegar. Season to taste with salt and freshly ground pepper.

GRILLED OYSTERS WITH TOMATILLO SALSA

Prepare a charcoal or gas grill for grilling over high heat. You may also use a broiler; preheat the broiler and line the bottom of a broiler pan with aluminum foil. Oil the grill rack or the top of the broiler pan with a paper towel soaked in oil.

To make the salsa, place the tomatillos and chile on the grill rack over direct heat or put them on the broiler pan and place about 3 inches (7.5 cm) from the heat source. Grill or broil until softened and slightly blackened, about 5 minutes on each side. Transfer the tomatillos to a blender. Remove the stem from the chile and add the chile and garlic to the blender. Purée to a coarse sauce. Transfer to a bowl and stir in the onion, cilantro, vinegar, and lime juice. Season with salt and pepper to taste and mix well. Divide among 4 small bowls. Set aside.

Arrange the oysters on the grill rack, rounded side down (to contain their liquor), and cover the grill, or place them on the prepared broiler pan and place the pan under the broiler 2–3 inches (5–7.5 cm) from the heat source. Cook until the oysters open, 4–8 minutes. Check once or twice during the cooking time and transfer any opened oysters to a bowl. Some oysters may open only slightly.

Place 4 oysters on each plate with a bowl of salsa in the center. Garnish with the cilantro sprigs and serve immediately, using an oyster knife to open the shells fully, if necessary. You may also remove the tops and serve on the half shell.

MAKES 4 FIRST-COURSE SERVINGS

TOMATILLOS

Called "green tomatoes" *(tomates verdes)* in Mexico because they are the same shape as the familiar red fruits, tomatillos are actually related to the ground cherry. Their texture is firm, and the fruit has a citruslike taste. Remove the papery husk and rinse to remove any sticky residue before using. Tomatillos are available year-round, but they are at their best in August through November. Look for them in specialty-produce markets and Latin groceries, and choose those that have just burst their husks. Drained canned tomatillos can also be used.

FOR THE TOMATILLO SALSA:

¾ lb (375 g) tomatillos, husked and rinsed *(far left)*

1 green serrano chile

2 cloves garlic

¼ cup (1 oz/30 g) finely diced white onion

½ cup (½ oz/15 g) packed fresh cilantro (fresh coriander) leaves

1 tablespoon seasoned rice vinegar

1 tablespoon fresh lime juice

Sea salt and freshly ground pepper

16 large oysters in the shell, scrubbed

Fresh cilantro (fresh coriander) sprigs for garnish

MIXED GRILL WITH ANCHOÏADE

Anchoïade *(far right)*

2 fresh or thawed frozen rock lobster tails, 8–10 oz (250–315 g) each

Extra-virgin olive oil for coating

Salt and freshly ground white pepper

1 lb (500 g) firm-fleshed fish fillets such as tuna or salmon

12 large sea scallops, trimmed if needed (page 108)

12 jumbo shrimp (prawns) in the shell

12 large black mussels, rinsed and debearded (page 13)

12 large hard-shell clams, rinsed

12 large oysters in the shell, scrubbed

Lemon wedges for garnish

Fresh flat-leaf (Italian) parsley sprigs for garnish

Thick slices French or Italian bread, grilled and brushed on one side with olive oil, for serving

Spicy Aioli (page 40) or Romesco Sauce (page 63) for serving (optional)

Prepare a grill for grilling over medium-high heat. Or, line the bottom of a broiler pan with aluminum foil. Soak 8 long wooden skewers in water to cover for 30 minutes; drain. Make the *anchoïade (right)*. Preheat the broiler, if using. Oil the grill rack or the top of the broiler pan with a paper towel soaked with oil.

Using a large chef's knife, cut the lobster tails in half down the center. Using kitchen shears, cut off the cartilage on the shell side of each piece of lobster. Coat the lobster tails on all sides with olive oil. Sprinkle the flesh side with salt and white pepper.

Cut the fish fillets into 1-inch (2.5-cm) cubes and thread them onto 4 of the skewers. Alternately thread 3 scallops and 3 shrimp onto each of the remaining 4 skewers. Brush the fish, scallops, and shrimp with olive oil and sprinkle with salt and pepper.

Place the mussels and clams, rounded side down, on the rack or pan, discarding any that do not close to the touch. Add the oysters, rounded side down. Place the fish and shellfish skewers on the grill rack or prepared broiler pan. If grilling, cover the grill. If broiling, place the pan under the broiler 2–3 inches (5–7.5 cm) from the heat source. Cook the shellfish skewers until the shrimp are evenly pink and the scallops opaque and lightly browned, about 1½ minutes per side. Cook the fish until opaque throughout, about 4 minutes on each side. Cook the oysters, mussels, and clams until they open, 4–6 minutes, discarding any that fail to open. Grill the lobster tails until the shells are red and the flesh is opaque throughout, about 3 minutes per side.

Transfer all the fish and shellfish to a warmed platter or 4 plates. Garnish with the lemons and parsley and serve immediately, with the bread and individual bowls of *anchoïade* and a second sauce, if you like, for dipping or spreading on the bread.

MAKES 4 MAIN-COURSE SERVINGS

ANCHOÏADE

This Provençal dipping sauce made with anchovies is also very good as a dip for crudités or roasted vegetables; made with less oil, it can be used as a spread for grilled bread. To make the *anchoïade* in a blender, combine ½ cup (4 fl oz/125 ml) extra-virgin olive oil, 2 cloves garlic, 4 oil-packed anchovies, ¼ cup (⅓ oz/10 g) minced flat-leaf (Italian) parsley, and 1 tablespoon lemon juice and purée until smooth. Pour into a small bowl and add freshly ground pepper to taste.

SOUPS AND STEWS

The versatility of seafood is highlighted in this chapter, with recipes that range from delicate soups to hearty stews, and that span the seasons, from an oyster stew for a winter meal to salmon chowder best enjoyed at the height of summer. Unlike many soups, those made from seafood need only brief cooking once the fish or shellfish are added, perfect for last-minute entertaining.

SEAFOOD BISQUE

In a small saucepan over medium heat, melt 3 tablespoons of the butter. Add the shallots and sauté until translucent, about 3 minutes. Add the shrimp, scallops, and crabmeat and sauté just until the scallops begin to turn opaque, about 2 minutes. Add the sherry and sauté for 1 minute longer. Remove from the heat and set aside.

In a separate saucepan over medium-low heat, melt the remaining 4 tablespoons butter. Stir in the flour to make a roux (see page 17) and cook, stirring constantly, for 2–3 minutes; do not let the mixture color. Gradually whisk in the vermouth and stock, then the half-and-half. Simmer, whisking occasionally, for about 15 minutes to develop the flavor and thicken slightly. Stir in the shellfish mixture and cook just to heat through, 1–2 minutes. Season with salt and white pepper to taste.

To serve, pour into warmed shallow bowls and garnish each with a little of the tarragon.

MAKES 4–6 FIRST-COURSE SERVINGS

FISH STOCK

A fish stock adds flavor to any seafood soup, stew, or sauce, though in some recipes, such as a light soup, you may prefer the mild flavor of chicken stock (page 111) or broth. Fish stock is easily made at home; make a habit of saving fish heads and parts, as well as lobster, shrimp, and crab shells, and freezing them in separate containers until you have enough to make stock (page 111). Good-quality frozen fish stock is available in specialty-food shops; it may be diluted to the desired strength.

Clam juice, widely available in bottles, is often substituted for fish stock, sometimes in combination with chicken stock.

---

7 tablespoons (3½ oz/105 g) unsalted butter

3 shallots, minced

6 oz (185 g) cooked cocktail shrimp

6 oz (185 g) bay scallops

6 oz (185 g) fresh lump crabmeat, picked over for shell fragments, or frozen crabmeat, drained

¼ cup (2 fl oz/60 ml) dry sherry or Marsala

¼ cup (1½ oz/45 g) all-purpose (plain) flour

½ cup (4 fl oz/125 ml) dry white vermouth or wine

4 cups (32 fl oz/1 l) fish stock or shrimp stock (page 111), or 2 cups (16 fl oz/500 ml) *each* bottled clam juice and chicken stock (page 111) or prepared low-sodium chicken broth

2 cups (16 fl oz/500 ml) half-and-half (half cream)

Sea salt and freshly ground white pepper

Minced fresh tarragon for garnish

MUSSEL SOUP WITH CREAM AND BRANDY

4 tablespoons (2 oz/60 g) unsalted butter

2 green (spring) onions, including tender green parts, finely chopped

½ cup (4 fl oz/125 ml) dry white vermouth or wine

4 cups (32 fl oz/1 l) chicken stock (page 111) or prepared low-sodium chicken broth

1½–2 lb (750 g–1 kg) large black mussels, rinsed and debearded (page 13)

¼ cup (1½ oz/45 g) all-purpose (plain) flour

¼ cup (2 fl oz/60 ml) brandy

½ cup (4 fl oz/125 ml) heavy (double) cream

Grated or minced zest and juice of 1 orange

Sea salt and freshly ground white pepper

Finely shredded fresh basil leaves or minced flat-leaf (Italian) parsley for garnish

In a soup pot, melt the butter over medium-low heat and stir in the green onions. Sauté until the white part of the onions is translucent, about 3 minutes. Whisk in the wine and cook for 1 minute. Whisk in the stock, raise the heat to medium-high, and bring to a boil. Reduce the heat to a simmer and add the mussels, discarding any that do not close to the touch. Cover the pan and cook until the mussels open, about 3 minutes. Using a slotted spoon, transfer the mussels to a bowl. Discard any mussels that do not open.

Using a ladle, transfer about 2 ladlefuls of the liquid to a small bowl and whisk in the flour until smooth. Return the mixture to the pot. Bring the liquid to a boil over high heat and whisk for 1 minute. Reduce the heat to a simmer and cook to develop the flavor and thicken slightly, about 10 minutes. Meanwhile, remove the mussels from the shells and discard the shells.

Just before serving, stir the brandy, cream, orange zest and juice, and sea salt and white pepper to taste into the soup. Return the mussel meats and any accumulated juices to the pot. Simmer just to heat the mussels through, about 1 minute. Serve immediately in warmed shallow bowls, garnished with the basil.

MAKES 4–6 MAIN-COURSE SERVINGS

CITRUS ZEST AND JUICE

When citrus zest and juice are both used in a recipe, it's easier to remove the zest, or thin colored layer of the rind, first. For grated zest, use a grater with a handle and small rasps, which is usually sharper and easier to use than a four-sided grater/shredder. A Microplane grater also works very well. Or, use a standard citrus zester, an implement with five or so small holes at the end that removes the zest in thin strips, as shown above, and then mince the thin strips. When a recipe calls for large strips of zest that need to be removed before serving, use a vegetable peeler.

SALMON AND CORN CHOWDER

Cut the salmon into 1-inch (2.5-cm) cubes. In a frying pan, melt 1 tablespoon of the butter with 1 tablespoon of the olive oil over medium heat. Add the salmon, in batches as needed to avoid crowding, and sauté just until opaque on the outside, about 2 minutes. Remove from the heat and set aside.

In a large saucepan over medium heat, melt the remaining 1 tablespoon butter with the remaining 1 tablespoon olive oil. Add the shallots and sauté until translucent, about 3 minutes. Add the stock. Raise the heat to high and bring the stock to a boil. Reduce the heat to a simmer and add the potatoes. Cover partially and cook until the potatoes are tender, about 15 minutes.

In a blender, combine ½ cup (3 oz/90 g) of the corn kernels with ½ cup (4 fl oz/125 ml) of the half-and-half. Purée until smooth. Add this mixture to the chowder. Add the remaining half-and-half and the remaining corn kernels and simmer until the corn is tender-crisp, about 5 minutes. Add the salmon and simmer just until barely cooked through, about 2 minutes. Season with salt and white pepper to taste.

Serve immediately in warmed soup bowls, garnished with the shredded basil.

MAKES 4 MAIN-COURSE SERVINGS

CUTTING KERNELS FROM THE COB

Holding an ear of corn by its pointed end, stand it upright and slightly angled, resting its stem end in the bottom of a wide bowl. Using a sharp knife, cut down the length of the cob, taking off 3 or 4 rows of kernels at a time and rotating the ear slightly with each cut. Cut as close to the cob as possible. Continue until all the kernels have been removed. To get as much juice as possible for a recipe that requires it, when all the kernels have been removed, stand the cob on end and scrape down with the dull side of the knife blade to draw out the remaining corn milk.

1 lb (500 g) salmon fillets, skin and pin bones removed

2 tablespoons unsalted butter

2 tablespoons extra-virgin olive oil

2 shallots, minced

4 cups (32 fl oz/1 l) chicken stock (page 111) or prepared low-sodium chicken broth

4 unpeeled red potatoes, cut into ½-inch (12-mm) dice

2 cups (12 oz/375 g) corn kernels (from about 4 ears)

1 cup (8 fl oz/250 ml) half-and-half (half cream)

Sea salt and ground white pepper

Shredded fresh basil for garnish

OYSTER STEW

3 tablespoons unsalted
butter

2 shallots, minced

4 stalks celery, including
leaves, finely diced

1 teaspoon celery seeds

¼ cup (2 fl oz/60 ml) dry
white vermouth or wine

1 cup (8 fl oz/250 ml) fish
stock (page 111) or bottled
clam juice

3 cups (24 fl oz/750 ml)
chicken stock (page 111)
or prepared low-sodium
chicken broth

Salt and freshly ground
white pepper

½ cup (4 fl oz/125 ml)
heavy (double) cream

30 oz (940 g) jarred
shucked small oysters
with their liquor (page 108)

½–1 teaspoon sweet
Hungarian paprika, or
to taste, plus extra for
garnish (optional)

Minced fresh flat-leaf
(Italian) parsley for garnish

In a soup pot over medium heat, melt 2 tablespoons of the butter. Add the shallots and sauté until translucent, about 3 minutes. Add the celery and celery seeds and sauté until the celery brightens in color, about 2 minutes. Stir in the vermouth and cook for 3–4 minutes to burn off some of the alcohol. Add the fish stock, chicken stock, and salt and white pepper to taste. Reduce the heat to low, cover, and simmer for about 15 minutes.

Add the cream and heat for 2–3 minutes. Add the oysters and cook, uncovered, until they have plumped up and their edges are curled, about 3 minutes. Stir in the remaining 1 tablespoon butter and paprika to taste. Taste and adjust the seasoning.

To serve, pour into warmed bowls and garnish each serving with a little paprika, if desired, and a sprinkling of the parsley.

Serving Tip: Serve slices of coarse country bread, grilled or toasted and brushed with melted butter, alongside the stew for dipping.

MAKES 4–6 MAIN-COURSE SERVINGS

CELERY AND CELERY SEEDS

The sweet-briny taste of fresh oysters is a natural with the crisp, light flavors of celery and sweet anise. This recipe uses celery stalks, celery seeds, and celery leaves to complement the oysters; the stalks and leaves add a slight crunchy texture, while the seeds underscore the clean celery flavor. Celery seeds are sold in bottles in the herb section of most supermarkets and specialty-food stores.

MEDITERRANEAN FISH STEW

SHELLING AND
DEVEINING SHRIMP
Beginning at the head end of
the shrimp, pull off the legs
and shell of the shrimp,
leaving the tail segments
attached, if desired. (Save the
shells and freeze them until
you accumulate enough to
make Shrimp Stock, page 111,
if you like.) The intestinal vein
in shrimp is edible but is often
removed for appearance's
sake, or in large shrimp
because it can occasionally
give a gritty texture. To devein
shrimp, using a paring knife,
make a shallow cut down the
outside curve of the shrimp.
Pull out the vein with the tip
of the knife and discard.

Finely chop the onion, celery stalk (including leaves), and carrot, and mince the garlic. Finely chop the anchovies. Drain and chop the tomatoes, reserving the juice. Toast and grind the saffron (page 36), then dissolve in 1 tablespoon hot water.

In a soup pot, heat 4 tablespoons (2 fl oz/60 ml) olive oil over medium heat. Add the onion, celery, and carrot and sauté until the onion is translucent, about 3 minutes. Add the garlic, thyme, red pepper flakes, and anchovies and sauté until the mixture is fragrant and the anchovies have melted, about 3 minutes. Add the wine and simmer until reduced by half, about 10 minutes. Add the tomatoes (but not their juice), fish stock, 1 cup (8 fl oz/ 250 ml) water, saffron mixture, bay leaf, and rosemary. Reduce the heat to medium-low and simmer for 15 minutes. Taste and adjust the seasoning. Add some of the reserved tomato juice if you want more liquid or more tomato flavor.

Just before serving, add the fish fillets, cover, and simmer just until opaque, about 2 minutes. Add the clams, discarding any that do not close to the touch, cover, and simmer until most of the clams open, about 6 minutes. Add the mussels, discarding any that do not close to the touch, cover, and cook until they open, 3–4 minutes. Discard any clams or mussels that do not open. Add the shrimp and cook, uncovered, just until pink, about 2 minutes. Remove from the heat and season with salt to taste.

Discard the bay leaf. Serve in warmed large bowls, sprinkled with the parsley and drizzled with a little olive oil.

Note: Snapper, lingcod, or tilapia is a good choice for this stew. Using homemade fish stock will make a difference in flavor; however, you can substitute 2 cups (16 fl oz/500 ml) bottled clam juice plus 2 cups chicken stock (page 111) or prepared low-sodium chicken broth.

MAKES 6 MAIN-COURSE SERVINGS

½ small yellow onion

1 stalk celery

1 carrot, peeled

3 cloves garlic

2 oil-packed anchovies

1 can (14½ oz/455 g) tomatoes

Pinch of saffron threads

Extra-virgin olive oil

1 teaspoon dried thyme

½ teaspoon red pepper flakes

1 cup (8 fl oz/250 ml) dry white vermouth or wine

4 cups (32 fl oz/1 l) fish stock (page 111) (see Note)

1 bay leaf

1 sprig fresh rosemary

2 lb (1 kg) firm white-fleshed fish fillets, cut into bite-sized pieces

12 littleneck or Manila clams, rinsed

12 black mussels, rinsed and debearded (page 13)

12 oz (375 g) large shrimp (prawns), shelled and deveined *(far left)*

Sea salt

3 tablespoons minced fresh flat-leaf (Italian) parsley

SPECIAL OCCASIONS

Certain kinds of seafood seem destined for celebrations: delicate and luxurious lobster, crab, and scallops are often chosen for holiday meals like New Year's Eve or for romantic dinners, but they can make any occasion special. From a classic clam appetizer to a dramatic steamed whole fish or boiled Maine lobster, the recipes in this chapter will please your guests.

CLAMS OREGANATA

To make dried bread crumbs, put the bread in a low (200°F/95°C) oven for 1 hour to dry out without browning. When the bread is dried, break it into chunks and process in a food processor or blender into fine crumbs, or place in a sturdy plastic bag and crush with a rolling pin. Measure out ¼ cup (1 oz/30 g) crumbs.

Preheat the broiler (grill). Strain the clam juices through a double thickness of dampened cheesecloth (muslin).

In each of 4 shallow, flameproof individual baking dishes place 6 of the reserved half shells and put a clam in each one. In a small bowl, combine the strained clam juices, olive oil, vinegar, garlic, and red pepper flakes. Whisk to blend. Spoon an equal amount, about 3 tablespoons, of the mixture over the clams in each dish.

In a small bowl, combine the bread crumbs, oregano, and marjoram and stir to blend. Drizzle lightly with olive oil and stir again to coat the crumbs. Sprinkle each clam with a large pinch of the bread crumb mixture. Place the dishes under the broiler about 3 inches (7.5 cm) from the heat source and broil until the crumbs are toasted and the clams are opaque, 1–2 minutes. Serve at once.

Serving Tip: Serve with thick slices of coarse country bread for dipping into the flavored oil, and a bowl of sea salt for sprinkling if desired (the clams will naturally be quite salty).

MAKES 4 FIRST-COURSE SERVINGS

SHUCKING CLAMS

Clams are easy to shuck, but to save time you can ask your fishmonger to shuck them for you, reserving the shells. To shuck them yourself, hold a clam knife or oyster knife in one hand and pick up a clam with your other hand, protected by a heavy glove or oven mitt. Holding the clam over a bowl to catch the juices, insert the blade of the knife between the shells at the point where they meet to make a heart shape on the bottom, then twist to open the shell. Sever the top connector muscle and break the top shell off. Sever the bottom connector muscle and drop the meat into the bowl.

1 slice country-style bread

24 littleneck or Manila clams, rinsed and shucked *(far left)*, juices and 24 deep half shells reserved

¼ cup (2 fl oz/60 ml) extra-virgin olive oil, plus more for drizzling

1 tablespoon red wine vinegar

1 clove garlic, minced

Pinch of red pepper flakes

1 tablespoon minced fresh oregano

1 tablespoon minced fresh marjoram or flat-leaf (Italian) parsley

SAUTÉED SCALLOPS WITH LEMON BEURRE BLANC

30 large sea scallops,
trimmed if needed
(page 108)

Sea salt and freshly
ground white pepper

Canola or grapeseed
oil for sautéing

FOR THE LEMON
BEURRE BLANC:

1 tablespoon fresh
lemon juice

1 tablespoon dry white
vermouth or wine

1 small shallot, minced

¾ cup (6 oz/185 g)
cold unsalted butter,
cut into 12 pieces

Salt and freshly ground
white pepper

Minced fresh chives
for garnish

Pat the scallops dry with paper towels. Season on both sides with salt and white pepper to taste. Coat the bottom of a large sauté pan with oil and heat over medium-high heat until the oil shimmers. Add the scallops, in batches as needed to avoid crowding, and sear on each side until lightly golden brown, about 1 minute on each side. Using a slotted metal spatula, transfer the scallops to a platter in a low (200°F/95°C) oven to keep warm.

To make the lemon *beurre blanc*, combine the lemon juice, vermouth, and shallot in small, heavy nonreactive saucepan. Bring to a low boil over medium-low heat and cook until the liquid is reduced to about 1 teaspoon. Remove the pan from the heat and, using a whisk, beat in 1 piece of butter, then a second piece. Place the pan over very low heat and whisk in the remaining butter one piece at a time to make an emulsified sauce. Remove from the heat and whisk in salt and white pepper to taste.

Pour the *beurre blanc* over the scallops and sprinkle liberally with the chives. Serve immediately.

MAKES 6 MAIN-COURSE SERVINGS

CANOLA OIL AND
GRAPESEED OIL
Canola oil and grapeseed
oil are both mild oils that
add little or no flavor of their
own to other foods. Canola
oil is high in healthful mono-
unsaturated fat, while grapeseed oil, which is less widely
available, is high in healthful
linoleic acid. Both can be
heated to high temperatures
for sautéing without burning.

CRAB AND SHRIMP SALAD WITH AVOCADO AND ORANGES

SEGMENTING ORANGES
Using a chef's knife, cut off the top and bottom of an orange down to the flesh. Stand the orange upright on the cutting board and use the knife to cut off the peel down to the flesh in vertical strips.

Holding the orange over a bowl, use the knife to cut on either side of the membranes to release the segments into the bowl. When all the segments have been released, squeeze the membranes to extract more juice.

To make the marinated onion, cut the onion crosswise into slices ⅛ inch (3 mm) thick. Place the slices in a small bowl and toss with the raspberry vinegar, kosher salt, and sugar. Let stand for about 30 minutes to soften and mellow the onion. Drain.

Meanwhile, place a collapsible steamer in a saucepan with about ½ inch water (the water should not touch the steamer) and bring to a simmer over medium-high heat. Add the shrimp, cover, reduce the heat to medium, and steam the shrimp until evenly pink, about 2 minutes, stirring once if necessary. Remove from the heat and let cool to the touch. Shell and devein the shrimp (page 86), leaving the tail segments intact if desired. Peel and segment the oranges, reserving the juice *(left)*.

To make the dressing, combine the olive oil, sherry vinegar, the ½ tablespoon lemon juice, 1 tablespoon of the reserved orange juice, and sea salt and white pepper to taste in a small bowl and whisk to blend. Taste and adjust the seasoning with a little more lemon juice if necessary.

In a large bowl, combine the watercress, lettuce, and cilantro sprigs. Add all but 2 tablespoons of the dressing and toss to combine. Transfer the salad greens to a large, shallow bowl or platter or 4 individual bowls. Arrange the crab, shrimp, orange segments, and avocado slices on top and drizzle the remaining dressing over them. Scatter the marinated onion over the salad and sprinkle with the orange zest. Serve immediately.

Variation Tip: Replace the oranges with 1 large mango; cut the flesh from the pit (page 60) and then peel the halves and cut them into slices. Replace the orange juice in the dressing with fresh lemon juice.

MAKES 4–6 LIGHT MAIN-COURSE SERVINGS

FOR THE MARINATED ONION:

1 small red onion

¼ cup (2 fl oz/60 ml) raspberry or red wine vinegar

Large pinch of kosher salt

Large pinch of sugar

12–18 large shrimp (prawns) in the shell

2 large navel oranges, plus the zest of 1 orange

6 tablespoons (3 fl oz/90 ml) extra-virgin olive oil

1 tablespoon sherry vinegar

½ tablespoon fresh lemon juice, or more to taste

Sea salt and white pepper

2 bunches watercress, stemmed

1 head red-leaf lettuce, leaves separated and torn into large pieces

1 handful fresh cilantro (fresh coriander) sprigs

8–12 oz (250–375 g) fresh lump crabmeat, picked over for shell fragments

1 large ripe avocado, pitted, peeled, and cut into lengthwise slices

LOBSTER RISOTTO WITH WHITE TRUFFLE OIL

5 cups (40 fl oz/1.25 l) lobster stock (page 111) (see Note)

2 fresh or thawed frozen rock lobster tails, about 10 oz (315 g) each *(far right)*

2 tablespoons unsalted butter

2 tablespoons extra-virgin olive oil

2 shallots, minced

2 cups (14 oz/440 g) Arborio rice

½ cup (4 fl oz/125 ml) dry white vermouth or wine

Sea salt and freshly ground white pepper

Snipped fresh chives for garnish

White truffle oil for drizzling

In a saucepan, bring the stock to a low boil over medium-high heat. Add the lobster tails, cover, and cook until opaque throughout, 5–6 minutes. Using tongs, transfer the lobster tails to a plate and let cool. Using kitchen shears and wearing heavy gloves, cut through the cartilage on each side of the bottom of each tail; beware of the sharp spines. Pull the meat out of the shell from the top. Cut the meat into ½-inch (12-mm) dice and set aside.

Return the stock to a simmer. In a wide, heavy saucepan over medium heat, melt the butter with the olive oil. Add the shallots and sauté until translucent, about 3 minutes. Add the rice and stir until well coated, about 3 minutes. Add the vermouth and stir until it is almost completely absorbed. Add ½ cup (4 fl oz/125 ml) of the simmering stock and stir until it is almost completely absorbed; a flat-bottomed wooden spatula is ideal for this. Continue to add the stock by ½-cup measures, stirring in each addition until it is almost completely absorbed. After 20 minutes, taste the risotto; when ready, it should be firm but tender. You may need to cook it 5–10 minutes longer, depending on the rice. If you have used all the stock, continue cooking by adding hot water ½ cup at a time until the risotto is done. Add sea salt and white pepper to taste. Stir in the lobster and cook for 1–2 minutes to heat it through. Add a last splash of stock or hot water if you like your risotto loose rather than sticky.

Serve immediately in warmed shallow bowls, garnished with the chives. Pass the truffle oil at the table.

Note: This risotto is ideally made with lobster stock (page 111), but you may also use shrimp stock (page 111), fish stock (page 111), thawed and diluted frozen prepared fish stock, or a mixture of half chicken stock (page 111) and half bottled clam juice.

MAKES 6 FIRST-COURSE OR 4 MAIN-COURSE SERVINGS

LOBSTER TAILS

Meaty and tender, lobster tails sold commercially come from the spiny, or rock, lobster. This lobster has no claws and more tail meat than the Maine lobster. Its fresh season is brief, so the tails are almost always sold frozen. Defrost them in the refrigerator overnight, or in a heavy-duty zippered plastic bag immersed in a bowl of cold water for about 4 hours. The best lobster tails are cold-water ones from Australia. If possible, ask your fishmonger to special-order these large lobster tails for you; the smaller ones sold in plastic bags in supermarkets will not yield as much meat.

GARLIC CRAB WITH SPAGHETTINI

Fill a large stockpot with enough water to cover the crab and bring to a boil over high heat. Fill a large bowl or the sink with cold water and ice cubes to make an ice bath. Stir ¼ cup (2 oz/60 g) kosher salt into the boiling water. Plunge the crab into the pot. Immediately cover the pot and listen to determine when the water returns to a full boil; this could take a few minutes. Reduce the heat to medium-high and cook Dungeness crab for 20 minutes, blue crabs for 10 minutes, counting from when the water returns to a boil. Use tongs to remove the crab from the pot. Transfer the crab to the ice bath and let cool for 10 minutes. Clean the cooked crab as described on pages 108–9, reserving the crab butter. Using a large chef's knife, cut the crab in half from top to bottom. Cut each half into sections, each with a leg or claw attached. Crack the legs and claws with a crab mallet, butcher steel, or hammer, but leave the meat in the shell.

Bring a large pot three-fourths full of water to a boil and add a generous amount of kosher salt. Add the pasta, stir well, and cook, stirring once or twice, until al dente, about 6 minutes.

Meanwhile, in a large frying pan, melt the butter with the olive oil over medium heat. Add the garlic and the red pepper flakes to taste and sauté until fragrant, about 1 minute. Add the crab pieces, meat still in the shell, and sauté until well coated and heated through, about 3 minutes. Stir in the reserved crab butter.

Drain the pasta and put it in a warmed bowl. Add the crab and toss. Add the lemon juice, parsley, and sea salt to taste; toss again. Serve at once. Accompany with lobster picks, skewers, or fish forks for removing the crabmeat from the shells, and provide finger bowls, plenty of napkins, and a plate for the empty shells.

Note: You may also make this dish with purchased cooked crab.

MAKES 4 MAIN-COURSE SERVINGS

GARLIC SAVVY

When buying garlic, choose plump, firm heads with no brown discolorations. To peel a clove of garlic, lightly crush the clove with the flat side of a chef's knife. Remove and discard the peel, then cut off the root and tip ends and slice or mince the clove. Especially during the winter months, look for and remove any green sprout that might be at the center of a clove before chopping it, as it can impart a bitter flavor. And always take care not to cook garlic beyond a light golden color, or it can taste harsh.

1 live Dungeness crab, about 2½ lb (1.25 kg), or 4 live hard-shell blue crabs (see Note), about 2 lb (1 kg) total weight

Kosher salt

1 lb (500 g) spaghettini pasta

4 tablespoons (2 oz/60 g) unsalted butter

½ cup (4 fl oz/125 ml) extra-virgin olive oil

6 large cloves garlic, minced

Red pepper flakes

2 tablespoons fresh lemon juice

½ cup (¾ oz/20 g) minced fresh flat-leaf (Italian) parsley for garnish

Sea salt

STEAMED WHOLE FISH WITH DIPPING SAUCE

1 whole sea bass, striped bass, or other fish with mild, sweet flesh, about 3 lb (1.5 kg), cleaned

½ tablespoon Chinese rice wine or dry sherry

Chile oil

One 1-inch (2.5-cm) piece fresh ginger, peeled and slivered

2 green (spring) onions, including tender green parts, cut into lengthwise slivers

FOR THE DIPPING SAUCE:

¼ cup (2 fl oz/60 ml) rice vinegar

1 tablespoon tamari or light soy sauce

1 tablespoon minced fresh cilantro (fresh coriander)

1 clove garlic, minced

Fresh cilantro (fresh coriander) sprigs for garnish

Rinse the fish and pat it dry with paper towels. Rub the inside of the fish with the wine and 2 or 3 dashes of chile oil. Sprinkle the ginger inside the fish and lay the slivered green onions inside as well.

In a large wok with a cover or a stockpot, bring 2 inches (5 cm) of water to a boil over high heat. Reduce the heat to a simmer. Place the fish on a plate and sprinkle the water in the pan lightly with chile oil. Place the plate with the fish on a trivet or a tic-tac-toe of chopsticks set in the wok, and cover the wok. If using a stockpot, place a small metal bowl in the pot and place the plate on the bowl; cover the stockpot. Cook the fish until opaque throughout, about 20 minutes.

Meanwhile, make the dipping sauce: Combine the vinegar, ¼ cup (2 fl oz/60 ml) water, the tamari, cilantro, and garlic and divide among 4 small bowls.

Serve the whole fish on a warmed platter, garnished liberally with the cilantro sprigs, and provide each diner with a small bowl of dipping sauce.

MAKES 4 MAIN-COURSE SERVINGS

TAMARI

Tamari refers to a traditional Japanese soy sauce that is made without wheat, although today that term is given to many Japanese-style soy sauces. Japanese "dark" soy sauce *(shoyu)* is equivalent to Chinese light soy sauce. Soy sauce and ginger often complement fish in both Chinese and Japanese cuisines.

BOILED MAINE LOBSTER WITH TWO DRAWN BUTTERS

DRAWN BUTTER
Drawn butter is simply butter that has been clarified by melting it and pouring, or "drawing," the clear yellow liquid off, separating it from the white foam and milky residue. Drawn, or clarified, butter is prized in cooking because it can be heated to a higher temperature than regular butter without burning; it can also be stored for months without turning rancid. Served hot, this appealing clear liquid butter is a traditional dipping sauce for lobster.

Fill a large stockpot with enough water to cover the lobsters and bring to a boil over high heat. Add the kosher salt. Meanwhile, remove the lobsters from the refrigerator; leave the rubber bands on the claws. (Do this in batches if needed.) Plunge the lobsters, head down, into the boiling water. Cover the pot and listen to determine when the water returns to a full boil; this could take 5 or 6 minutes. Reduce the heat to medium-high and cook 1¼-lb lobsters for 9–10 minutes and 1½-lb lobsters for 10–11 minutes, counting from when the water returns to a boil.

Meanwhile, make the drawn butters: In a small saucepan, melt the butter over low heat. Remove from the heat and let stand for 2–3 minutes. Pour off the clear yellow melted butter, dividing it between 2 small bowls and leaving the white milk solids in the bottom of the saucepan. Add the lemon juice, dill, and sea salt to taste to one bowl; add the paprika and sea salt to taste to the other. Stir both mixtures. Place both bowls of drawn butter in a low (200°F/95°C) oven to keep warm.

Using tongs, remove the lobsters from the pot and rinse under cold running water for a few seconds. Remove any rubber bands from the claws. To drain, plunge a knife into the head of each lobster, between the eyes, and hold the lobster over the sink, holding it up first by the tail, then by the claws, and then by the tail again.

Serve each lobster on a large plate. Garnish with the dill sprigs and lemon wedges. Divide each drawn butter among 4 ramekins and serve one or both with each lobster. Accompany each lobster with a large napkin, a finger bowl, a lobster or nut cracker, kitchen shears, and lobster picks, nutpicks, or fish forks. Place a bowl in the center of the table for discarded shells.

MAKES 4 MAIN-COURSE SERVINGS

4 live Maine lobsters,
1¼–1½ lb (625–750 g) each

¼ cup (2 oz/60 g) kosher
salt

FOR THE LEMON-DILL AND
PAPRIKA DRAWN BUTTERS:

1 cup (8 oz/250 g)
unsalted butter

Juice of ½ lemon,
or to taste

1 tablespoon minced
fresh dill

Sea salt

1 teaspoon sweet or hot
Hungarian paprika or
pimentón picante (page 31)

Fresh dill sprigs for garnish

Lemon wedges for garnish

SEAFOOD BASICS

Seafood is prized for its freshness and delicacy, and the aim of the good cook is to preserve these characteristics from store to table. This section includes the basic information you will need to buy and prepare most kinds of fish and shellfish, along with a list of seafood equipment, tips on cooking and serving seafood, and basic recipes such as fish stock and shellfish stock.

ABOUT FISH

Quick to cook, low in fat, and rich in flavor, fish is an almost perfect food. The many kinds of fish can be divided into saltwater or freshwater, round or flat, and lean or oily. The types of fish most commonly found in the kitchen are round fish with mild, white flesh, such as halibut and red snapper; flat fish that are eaten whole or in fillets, such as flounder; and round fish that are higher in fat and have a meaty texture, such as mackerel, salmon, and tuna. Fishes in the same category can often be substituted for one another in recipes.

When shopping, look for fish with bright eyes, no detectable fishy odor, and flesh that is firm to the touch. Plan to cook all fresh fish within 24 hours, and store it in its original wrapping in the coldest part of the refrigerator. If refrigerating the fish overnight, it is best to put the package in a zippered plastic bag and store it on top of ice cubes placed in a baking dish, or simply place the package on top of frozen ice-substitute packs. Remove the seafood from the refrigerator about 30 minutes before cooking.

SKINNING FILLETS

Most fillets are sold already skinned, although fish with relatively thick skin, such as salmon, is usually sold with the skin still on. In many cases, it's a good idea to cook the fillets with the skin attached, as it helps to hold the flesh together, and the fatty skin also helps to keep the fish moist. If you prefer to serve the fish with the skin removed, simply remove it after cooking. You can also cut the flesh away from the skin while eating it.

REMOVING PIN BONES

Salmon, halibut, and several other types of fish fillets have pin bones, which stick into the fish like straight pins and should be removed before cooking. Run your fingers over the top of the fillet at its thickest part; you should feel the bones, which will be slightly off center and extend down into the fish at an angle. Using fish tweezers, or clean needle-nosed pliers or regular tweezers, pull each pin bone in the direction in which it slants to remove it. Also check the cut ends of the fillets and remove any small bones protruding there.

HEALTH BENEFITS OF FISH

All fish are high in protein and digestibility and most are low in fat. Those that are not, such as salmon, are high in the healthful omega-3 fatty acids that help to lower cholesterol. For these reasons, many nutritionists advise eating fish at least twice a week. Recently, however, the high mercury content of some fish has caused alarm, and fishmongers have been cautioned to list the mercury content of the fish that they sell. Fish high in mercury include swordfish, tilefish, King mackerel, and shark. These fish should not be eaten by pregnant women; nursing mothers, young children, and anyone who may become pregnant may want to avoid them as well. Salmon are not included in this category, but farmed salmon can be high in toxins; select wild salmon whenever possible.

ENDANGERED FISH

A number of the most popular kinds of fish are now considered endangered because of overfishing or pollution; they include Chilean sea bass, swordfish, orange roughy, and cod. Lists of endangered fish do occasionally change, and online resources such as the Monterey Bay Aquarium's Seafood Watch are available. Because so many types of fish are available, there is no need to purchase endangered fish. Ask the fishmonger about types to substitute.

ABOUT SHELLFISH

Shellfish can be divided into two major categories: crustaceans and mollusks. Crustaceans, which include crabs, lobsters, and shrimp, have long, jointed bodies with exoskeletons, while mollusks might have one shell (abalone and snails), two shells (clams, oysters, scallops), or no shell at all (squid, octopus). Many fresh shellfish, such as clams, lobsters, mussels, oysters, and crabs, are live when purchased; they should not be enclosed in plastic bags or submerged in water, or they will die.

SHRIMP

Shrimp (prawns) range in color from brown, gray, or white to striped or spotted. They vary in size from tiny cooked cocktail, or bay, shrimp to the much larger jumbo shrimp, which, along with large shrimp, are often called prawns in the United States. They are classified by size according to the number of shrimp per pound (500 g): miniature (100), medium (25–30), large (16–20), and jumbo (10–15). Look for plump, firm, fresh-smelling shrimp in the shell; the freshest shrimp will still have their heads. Frozen shrimp is usually better quality than shrimp that has been frozen and thawed. Plan to cook fresh shrimp within 24 hours, and store them in their original wrapping in the coldest part of the refrigerator. If refrigerating shrimp overnight, put the package in a zippered plastic bag and store on top of ice cubes placed in a baking dish, or simply place the package on top of frozen ice packs. Thaw frozen shrimp in the refrigerator, or in a heavy-duty zippered plastic bag submerged in cold water. To shell and devein shrimp, see page 86.

LOBSTER

Choose lively lobsters that arch their back and flap their tail vigorously when picked up. They should be wrapped in damp newspaper and kept in an open paper bag for transport and storage in the refrigerator. Cook them within 24 hours.

Preparing live lobsters: The most humane method of killing live lobsters is to plunge them head first into boiling water; this kills them quickly. If you plan to cut up the lobster before cooking it, plunge it into boiling water first and leave just until limp, about 1 minute.

Cleaning lobsters: Shown opposite are the basic steps in cleaning lobster and removing its meat after cooking:

1 Twist the tail to detach it from the body and break off the end flaps.

2 Use kitchen shears to cut along the length of the cartilage over the tail meat, spread the shell open, and extract the meat in one piece.

3 Pull the body out of the chest shell, then discard the white gills on the underside.

4 Break the chest in half and use a pick or fork to get at the meat between the cartilage; you can also eat the white matter, the green tomalley (liver), and any red roe that may be present if the lobster is female.

5 Remove and discard the dark intestinal vein that runs under the body to the end of the tail; also remove and discard the greenish stomach sac on one side of the head.

6 Break off the claws and their joints; crack the joints and dig out the meat, then bend the smaller claw backward to pull it off, and dig out its meat. Crack the large claws to extract the meat. Break off the legs, twist apart at the joints, and pull out the meat.

CLAMS

Clams may be either hard or soft shelled; "soft" shells are still quite firm, though thin and brittle. Soft-shell clams include East Coast steamer clams and geoduck; hard-shell clams include littlenecks and Manila clams. Soft-shell clams may be slightly open, while hard-shell clams are usually tightly closed; if not, they should close when the muscle is pricked with a knife. Store fresh clams in the refrigerator, wrapped in paper or placed in a bowl and covered with a cloth, and prepare them within 24 hours of purchase. To refrigerate clams overnight, place them on top of frozen ice-substitute packs. Although foraged clams tend to be sandy and must be soaked in saltwater before using, most commercially raised clams can simply be rinsed under cold running water, and scrubbed lightly with a brush if they appear sandy. To shuck clams, see page 90.

OYSTERS

Oysters are available year-round, but they are at their best during the winter months. Live oysters in the shell should be tightly closed when purchased. If you can't bring them straight home from the fishmonger's, bring an ice chest to transport them in. Store them in the refrigerator, rounded side down and covered with a damp towel, for up to 3 days. For preparations such as stews, look for shucked oysters sold in glass jars in the meat and fish departments of many supermarkets; use them within 24 hours.

If you need shucked fresh oysters with the shell but are short on time, call the fishmonger in advance and ask him or her to shuck the oysters and reserve them on the half shell right before you pick them up on the day you plan to serve them. Bring them straight home and refrigerate them, covered in plastic, in the cold rear bottom of the refrigerator, and serve within 3–4 hours.

SCALLOPS

These delicate morsels come in two varieties: large sea scallops, which are 1–2 inches (2.5–5 cm) in diameter, and small bay scallops, which are about ½ inch (12 mm) in diameter. Sea scallops are preferred for sautéing and grilling, while bay scallops are a good choice for soups and sauces. Fresh East Coast sea scallops are often labeled as "day-boat" or "diver" scallops; these designations mean that the scallops have not been frozen (a "day boat" returns to shore within 24 hours, so the scallops don't need to be preserved by freezing). The larger Atlantic sea scallops may be labeled "dry pack" or "chemical free." In either case, look for scallops that are not sitting in liquid, as some are soaked in phosphates to keep them plump. Scallops should be ivory in color, not white, and they may be somewhat misshapen rather than perfect rounds. Trim off any hard connective tissue on the side of the scallops before cooking.

CRABS

Buy live crabs the day you plan to cook them, or no more than 24 hours before cooking. Store them, wrapped in newspaper in an open paper bag, in the bottom of your refrigerator. If you must cut up a live crab, stun it first: Place the crab on a work surface with the head facing away from you and grasp the legs and claws on each side with each of your hands. Pick up the crab and strike the bottom of the crab shell, in the center, sharply on the edge of a counter or table. An alternative is to kill and partially cook the crab by plunging it into boiling water until limp, about 1 minute.

To clean a hard-shell crab after cooking, pull off and discard the eyes and mouth parts. Pull off the top shell and reserve it. Remove and discard the gills, which are the white feather-shaped pieces on each side of the body above the legs. Pull out and discard the firm, crooked white intestine along the center of the back. Turn the crab on its back and pull off the small triangular "breastplate" at the top. Spoon out and reserve the white and yellow "butter" in the body. Reach inside the reserved top shell and pull out the crab butter in the corners; reserve to use in your recipe.

SQUID

Squid, also called by its Italian name, calamari, is considered a mollusk, though it has no shell. It is harvested from spring to early fall on the northern Pacific Coast, and from winter to spring on the southern Pacific Coast. Squid is sold either whole or already cleaned; cleaned squid are often missing their tentacles as well as their ink sacs, but they are convenient to use. Squid should either be cooked very quickly, or stewed or braised until tender; otherwise they will tend to be rubbery and chewy.

To clean squid, first cut off the tentacles just above the eyes. Squeeze the hard, round beak from the end of the tentacles. Holding the tail end of the body flat on a cutting board with one hand, scrape the side of a chef's knife along the body, pressing hard to remove the innards. Holding down the tail end, pull out the long

quill protruding from the body. Rinse the squid well inside and out under running cold water. The skin does not need to be removed. If a recipe calls for rings, slice the body crosswise.

SEAFOOD EQUIPMENT

Use ceramic or glass bowls or dishes for marinating fish, as uncoated metal can give fish a metallic taste. Choose oval or round gratin dishes made of enameled cast iron, ceramic, or ovenproof glass—either large or in individual sizes—for cooking creamy fish and shellfish dishes. The large dishes are also useful for marinating and roasting seafood. If you plan to poach a large fish, a fish poacher is almost essential, although fillets can simply be poached in a small roasting pan or large frying pan of barely simmering water. A wok or large steamer is necessary for steaming whole fish. For sautéing fish, many people prefer nonstick, although fish shouldn't stick to the pan if the pan is hot and the fish is well coated with oil or flour.

Needle-nosed pliers or fish tweezers are the best tools for removing pin bones, though regular tweezers can also be used. Two large offset spatulas are useful for transferring whole fish or whole fillets to and from the pan. A fish spatula is an offset spatula with a long, thin, flexible slotted blade

designed specifically for transferring delicate fish fillets to and from the pan. A large fish-shaped wire basket with a handle is invaluable for grilling a whole fish, and either bamboo skewers or a grill basket is needed for grilling smaller pieces of fish and shellfish such as shrimp and scallops.

SHELLFISH TOOLS

Though you can make do with dull paring knives, screwdrivers, hammers, pliers, and oven mitts, using the right tools makes serving and eating crab, lobster, clams, and oysters easier. Some fishmongers and many kitchenware stores carry these tools:

Clam knife: A knife with a short, thick blade that is rounded on the end and sharp on one side.

Oyster knife: A knife with a short, thick blade that is pointed but dull on the end and dull on both sides.

Crab mallet: A wooden mallet for cracking crab legs; a hammer may also be used if you handle it gently.

Lobster and crab picks: Long, narrow metal tools with two tiny prongs on one end, used for digging meat out of nooks and corners of the shells.

Lobster cracker: A two-handled metal tool similar to pliers, used for cracking lobster claws and legs.

Shelling glove: A heavy rubber or metal glove used to protect your hand when shelling oysters and clams.

COOKING SEAFOOD

Seafood can be cooked in a number of ways, but one rule applies to every method, from grilling to roasting to frying: Don't overcook it. Most fish is done when it is opaque throughout; when the fish is prodded with a fork the juices should run milky white. The two exceptions are salmon, which is best cooked only until it is still translucent in the center, and ahi tuna, which is usually cooked only until rare or medium-rare. The rule established years ago by the Canadian fishing board calls for cooking at 350°F (180°C) for 8–10 minutes per inch (2.5 cm) of thickness; measure the fish at its thickest point before cooking and calculate the cooking time using this measurement. Lobster turns a bright red when cooked, while crab turns a bright orange. Shrimp are done when they are an even pink on both sides. Squid should be cooked either very briefly—until just opaque (and lightly browned if grilled or sautéed)—or for a relatively long period of time, to avoid toughness.

Remove seafood, especially fillets and whole fish, from the refrigerator 30 minutes before cooking. The seafood will cook more evenly if it is at room temperature.

GRILLING

The grill rack of charcoal and gas grills should always be scrubbed clean with a wire brush so that food won't stick to it. Also oil the grill rack before cooking. Fish and shellfish should be placed 5–6 inches (13–15 cm) above the hot coals (many grills have immovable grill racks fixed at 6 inches/15 cm from the fuel bed). To judge the heat of a charcoal fire, use the following cues: A hot fire will glow red through a light coat of white ash; a medium fire will barely glow orange through a thick coat of white ash; the coals of a low fire will have no visible red or orange glow, but instead a solid coat of gray ash.

SERVING SEAFOOD

Because seafood cooks so quickly, it is best to cook fish and shellfish immediately before serving; if it is not served as soon as it is done, it can dry out, or, if it is held in liquid, it can overcook. Most fish and shellfish are not good candidates for reheating, although fish baked in a cream sauce can sometimes be reheated successfully. Serve all cooked fish and shellfish on warmed platters or plates, as the delicate flesh cools quickly.

When serving crab and lobster, it is helpful to provide large napkins or even bibs to keep spatters caused by cracking and eating from the shells off of clothes. Finger bowls are also essential when serving these dishes, as are individual sauce bowls. Some other fish dishes, such as steamed whole fish with a dipping sauce, will also require small sauce bowls. Crab should be cracked in the kitchen before serving, using a wooden mallet or hammer, but either lobster or crab picks or fish forks should be served with it at the table; serve whole lobster with a lobster cracker or pliers, as well as lobster picks.

BASIC RECIPES

Here are several basic recipes that are used in some of the dishes in this book.

CHICKEN STOCK

4 fresh flat-leaf (Italian) parsley sprigs

1 fresh thyme sprig

1 bay leaf

6 lb (3 kg) chicken necks and backs

3 stalks celery, halved

3 carrots, peeled and halved

2 yellow onions, halved

2 leeks, white and light green parts only, cleaned (page 114) and sliced

Salt and freshly ground pepper

Wrap the parsley, thyme, and bay leaf in a piece of cheesecloth (muslin) and secure with kitchen string to make a bouquet garni.

In a large stockpot, combine the bouquet garni, chicken necks and backs, celery, carrots, onions, and leeks. Add enough cold water to just cover the ingredients (about 14 cups/3.5 l). Slowly bring to a boil over medium heat. Reduce the heat as low as possible and simmer, uncovered, for 3 hours, skimming off the foam that rises to the surface. Season with salt and pepper to taste.

Strain the stock into a bowl through a fine-mesh sieve. Let cool. Pour into airtight containers and refrigerate for at least 30 minutes or up to overnight. Remove the hardened fat from the surface and discard, then refrigerate for up to 3 days or freeze for up to 3 months. Makes about 3 qt (3 l).

STEAMED WHITE RICE

Sea salt

2 cups (14 oz/440 g) long-grain white rice

In a saucepan, bring 4 cups (32 fl oz/1 l) water to a boil. Add 1 teaspoon sea salt, then stir in the rice. Reduce the heat to low, cover, and simmer until all the water is absorbed and the rice is tender, about 20 minutes. Remove from the heat and let stand, covered, for at least 5 minutes. Fluff with a fork before serving. Makes 4 servings.

FISH STOCK

4 fresh flat-leaf (Italian) parsley sprigs

1 fresh thyme sprig

1 bay leaf

¼ cup (2 fl oz/60 ml) extra-virgin olive oil

1 yellow onion, coarsely chopped

1 carrot, peeled and coarsely chopped

2 stalks celery, coarsely chopped

½ cup (4 fl oz/125 ml) dry white wine

2 lb (1 kg) fish bones and parts from white-fleshed fish

Salt and freshly ground pepper

Wrap the parsley, thyme, and bay leaf in a piece of cheesecloth (muslin) and secure with kitchen string to make a bouquet garni.

In a large stockpot over medium heat, heat the olive oil. Add the onion, carrot, and celery and sauté until softened, 4–5 minutes. Add the wine and deglaze the pot, stirring to scrape up any browned bits from the bottom. Raise the heat to medium-high and cook until the wine is almost completely evaporated. Add 4 qt (4 l) water, the fish bones and parts, and the bouquet garni and bring to a boil. Reduce the heat to low and simmer, uncovered, for 30 minutes. Taste and season with salt and pepper.

Strain the stock into a bowl through a fine-mesh sieve and discard the solids. Let cool. Pour into airtight containers and refrigerate for up to 2 days or freeze for up to 2 months. Makes about 3 qt (3 l).

Shrimp Stock: Follow the above recipe, replacing the fish bones and parts with about 8 cups (8 oz/250 g) shrimp (prawn) shells.

Lobster Stock: Follow the recipe for fish stock, replacing the fish with the shells of 2 cooked lobsters, broken with a hammer.

GLOSSARY

BUTTER, UNSALTED Salt is added to butter to keep it fresher longer, but unsalted butter has a cleaner, sweeter taste. To store unsalted butter that won't be used within a week or so, wrap it in freezer-weight plastic and freeze.

CAPERS These buds of a Mediterranean bush, preserved in brine, add a burst of piquant flavor to mild foods such as fish. Drain and rinse capers before using.

CAYENNE PEPPER Ground dried red cayenne chiles yield a bright orange-red powder that adds spark to many savory dishes. Use just a tiny amount at first and then increase it according to your taste, as it is a powerful ingredient.

CHILES The heat of fresh chiles contrasts with the mild, sweet flavor of seafood. When cutting chiles, avoid touching your face. When done, wash the knife and work surface with hot, soapy water.

Serrano: Fresh serranos, which may be either red or green, are very hot. They are about 1½ inches (4 cm) long and have a blunt end.

Jalapeño: Fresh jalapeños, which also may be either red or green, range from hot to very hot. They are usually slightly longer and narrower than serranos.

CHINESE RICE WINE Similar in color and flavor to dry sherry, which can be used as a substitute, Chinese rice wine is available in Asian markets and many supermarkets. The best-quality rice wine is from eastern China and is named after the town of Shaoxing.

CHIVES These brilliant green grasslike spears lend color and a mild onion flavor when minced and added to savory dishes. The minced green tops of green onions may be substituted.

CILANTRO Also called fresh coriander or Chinese parsley, this green herb has delicate scalloped leaves and a unique, bright flavor. It is a favorite in Asian, Mexican, and Middle Eastern cuisines, and it is frequently served with fish. Store in the refrigerator with the ends submerged in a glass of water and a plastic bag placed over the top.

CITRUS Fish and citrus seem meant to go together: The tang of lemon and other citrus heightens the subtle flavor of fish.

Tangerine: Although the tangerine is only one kind of mandarin orange, the name is commonly give to a number of small to large varieties of mandarin, all of which have loose, easily peeled skin and an intense flavor. Tangerines are best in late winter and early spring.

Blood orange: The depth of the rosy blush on the outside and the light to deep red color on the inside varies, but all blood oranges have a sweet-tart raspberry-orange flavor. Look for them in late winter and early spring.

Valencia orange: A juice orange, the Valencia is usually available year-round, but it is at its best during winter.

CRÈME FRAÎCHE Traditional French crème fraîche is made from matured unpasteurized cream; the natural fermentation gives it a faintly sour taste similar to that of sour cream. Look for crème fraîche in the dairy section of your market.

CUMIN An aromatic seed, cumin is used in Indian, Mexican, and Middle Eastern cuisines to lend a nutty, smoky flavor to food. It is available in whole form or ground.

EGG, RAW Uncooked eggs carry a risk of being infected with salmonella, which can lead to food poisoning. This risk is of most concern to young children, older people, pregnant women, and anyone with a compromised immune system. If you have health and safety concerns, do not consume raw egg; you can seek out a pasteurized egg product to replace it.

FISH TYPES
Bass, sea: The large saltwater bass family includes groupers, black bass, striped bass, blue-nose bass, and white sea bass; all of them have tender, mild white flesh.

Although Chilean sea bass is endangered, white sea bass from California is commonly available. Blue-nose bass, which comes from Antarctica, is also available year-round.

Catfish: A freshwater fish from the American South, catfish is featured in soul food and Cajun cuisine. It is often fried or rubbed with a dried-spice mixture and "blackened" in a frying pan with very little oil.

Cod, rock: The rock cod is actually a rockfish; like true red snapper, from the Atlantic, and Pacific red snapper (actually rockfish), it has a mild white flesh and can be cooked in a wide variety of ways.

Halibut: A large flatfish found in both the Atlantic and Pacific Oceans; Atlantic halibut is much larger, up to 300 pounds (150 kg). Halibut has a mild, lean white flesh that lends itself to poaching, baking, and steaming.

Lingcod: Though not a true cod, lingcod has a dense, mild flesh that is good for broiling, grilling, and poaching. It also holds its shape in soups and stews.

Mahimahi: A fish found in tropical waters around the world; much of it is harvested near Hawaii. Mahimahi has a dense, sweet flesh with a moderate fat content, which makes it a good candidate for grilling.

Rockfish: What is called red snapper on the West Coast is actually a kind of rockfish that resembles red snapper. Pacific red snapper and other kinds of rockfish, such as rock cod, are interchangeable. Rockfish are found in many varieties on the Pacific Coast; they have a mild white flesh and may be cooked by almost any method, including grilling and broiling.

Salmon: The several varieties of salmon include chinook, or king, and coho, or silver. Born in freshwater, it lives in the ocean, then returns to its birthplace to spawn. Valued for its deep-colored, dense flesh, salmon has been overfished. Although salmon is widely farmed, there are concerns about the effects of salmon farming on the environment and the quality of the fish itself. Whenever possible, choose wild salmon, which is high in heart-healthy oil and naturally fed.

Snapper, red: True red snapper is from the Atlantic Ocean and has been dangerously overfished. "Red snapper" sold elsewhere is often actually rockfish. Both fish have a mild white flesh.

Sole: This is the name used for many members of the flatfish family, which have both eyes on one side of the head. Most fish identified as sole, such as petrale sole, lemon sole, sand dabs, and rex sole, are actually flounders. They are interchangeable in recipes, although sand dabs are smaller than others.

Tilapia: This fish from Costa Rica and Colombia is widely farmed elsewhere and is commonly available.

Trout: A freshwater fish with a wonderfully sweet, white flesh, trout is widely available whole, boned, or in fillets. Look also for pink-fleshed trout.

Tuna: The varieties of this large fish include albacore; ahi, or yellowfin; bluefin; and bonito. All have a dense, meaty flesh that ranges in color from light (albacore) to very dark (bonito). Ahi tuna is known for its dark red color and rich flavor.

FOCACCIA This dense, spongy Italian flat bread makes great sandwiches, used either fresh or toasted. Look for plain or herbed focaccia in Italian bakeries or delis, or specialty-foods stores. It is best the day it is baked, but it freezes well and can be refreshed by toasting.

GINGER This knobby rhizome is a classic accompaniment to fish, especially in Asian cuisines. Look for firm ginger with no discoloration. To peel ginger, cut off a small piece and use the edge of a large spoon to peel the skin. Use a chef's knife to cut the ginger into thin slices; to grate, use a ceramic ginger grater or a metal grater with small rasps, or chop finely with a chef's knife.

LEEKS This elongated cousin of the onion has a mild, buttery taste when cooked. Because leeks are grown in mounds of soil and their many layers easily trap dirt, take care to wash them well: Either cut the leek in half lengthwise and rinse it under cold running water while separating the leaves, or chop the leek before washing it in a bowl of water. The green leaves are tough; only the white and sometimes the light green parts are used in most recipes.

MARJORAM Similar in taste to oregano, but with a milder and sweeter flavor, marjoram is available fresh in many supermarkets and produce stores. It is also easily grown at home.

MARSALA This fortified Sicilian wine comes in dry and sweet versions. The dry wine is typically used in savory dishes.

NONREACTIVE Uncoated aluminum or cast-iron pans can discolor some foods made with acidic ingredients such as eggs or lemon juice. When in doubt, choose stainless steel, coated aluminum, or enameled cast iron.

OIL TYPES
Canola: See page 93.

Chile oil (Asian): This bottled oil, available in Asian markets and many supermarkets, has had hot red chiles steeped in it. It can be refrigerated indefinitely after opening.

Extra-virgin olive: The first cold pressing of olives yields this, the olive oil lowest in acid. It is also the purest of all olive oils, with a full, fruity flavor. It can be used in all phases of cooking, but save estate-bottled oils for salad dressings and other preparations that are not heated, and use less expensive ones for sautéing and frying.

Grapeseed: See page 93.

Peanut: Oil made from peanuts can be heated to quite a high temperature before it begins to smoke, and so is good for stir-frying and deep-frying. It is traditionally used in Chinese cuisine.

Sesame, Asian: Unlike clear sesame oil, which is made from raw white sesame seeds, Asian, or toasted, sesame oil is dark in color and intense in flavor because it is made with toasted sesame seeds. Use it sparingly.

PARSLEY, FLAT-LEAF (ITALIAN) Characterized by its large, serrated, flat leaves, flat-leaf parsley has a more pronounced flavor than curly-leafed parsley.

PEPPER, WHITE Black peppercorns that are soaked to remove their skins become white peppercorns, which are prized by many cooks because they have a milder flavor and their pale color is more pleasing in light-colored foods.

SALT, KOSHER Kosher salt is favored by many cooks because it has no additives and because its coarse grains are easy to pick up and impart a pure, salty flavor.

SALT, SEA Gathered from salt pans on the edge of the sea, sea salt has no additives and is preferred by many cooks for its clean, natural taste. It comes in both fine and coarse grinds; choose fine sea salt for adding to most foods. Sea salt has a natural affinity with fish.

SHERRY, DRY This fortified wine, originally from Spain, ranges in color

and sweetness from dry, or *fino,* sherry to sweet, or *oloroso.* Dry sherry is pale gold, with a light, nutty flavor.

TRUFFLE OIL Tiny bottles of olive oil infused with the flavor of milder white or more intense black truffles are imported from Italy. Drizzle lightly over cooked foods such as risotto and pasta to add the earthy flavor of this prized fungus.

VERMOUTH This fortified wine is available in sweet and red, sweet and white, or dry and white varieties. Dry white vermouth is an ingredient in the classic martini, and it may also be used in cooking. Because of its herbal aroma, it complements fish dishes. Substitute it in any recipe calling for dry white wine.

VINEGAR Keeping a variety of vinegars on hand allows you to make use of their subtly varying flavors in seafood dishes.

Balsamic: This Italian vinegar is made from boiled grape must. Aging in wooden barrels gives it a sweet undertone; the longer it is aged, the thicker the liquid and the higher the quality of the vinegar.

Champagne: White wine vinegar made with Champagne grapes is lighter and milder than most white wine vinegars.

Rice: A delicate, fragrant vinegar made from fermented rice. Seasoned rice vinegar has had salt and sugar added to it.

Sherry: Vinegar made from sherry has a delicate golden hue and a nutty flavor.

INDEX

SIMON & SCHUSTER SOURCE
A division of Simon & Schuster, Inc.
Rockefeller Center
1230 Avenue of the Americas
New York, NY 10020

WILLIAMS-SONOMA
Founder and Vice-Chairman: Chuck Williams

WELDON OWEN INC.
Chief Executive Officer: John Owen
President and Chief Operating Officer: Terry Newell
Vice President, International Sales: Stuart Laurence
Creative Director: Gaye Allen
Series Editor: Sarah Putman Clegg
Designer: Marisa Kwek
Production Director: Chris Hemesath
Color Manager: Teri Bell
Co-edition and Reprint Coordinator: Todd Rechner

Weldon Owen wishes to thank the following
people for their generous assistance and support
in producing this book: Copy Editor and Proofreader
Sharron Wood; Consulting Editor Sharon Silva;
Food and Prop Stylists Kim Konecny and Erin Quon;
Photographer's Assistant Faiza Ali; Production Editor
Joan Olson; Proofreader Carrie Bradley; and
Indexer Ken DellaPenta.

Set in Trajan, Utopia, and Vectora.

Williams-Sonoma Collection *Seafood* was
conceived and produced by Weldon Owen Inc.,
814 Montgomery Street, San Francisco,
California 94133, in collaboration with
Williams-Sonoma, 3250 Van Ness Avenue,
San Francisco, California 94109.

A Weldon Owen Production

For information regarding special discounts for
bulk purchases, please contact Simon & Schuster
Special Sales at 1-800-456-6798 or
business@simonandschuster.com

Color separations by Bright Arts Graphics
Singapore (Pte.) Ltd.
Printed and bound in Singapore by Tien Wah
Press (Pte.) Ltd.

First printed in 2005.

10 9 8 7 6 5

Library of Congress Cataloging-in-Publication
data is available.

ISBN 0-7432-6188-7